Theory
Solution-Focused
Practice

description and theory and description or theory
description or theory and theory or description
description or theory or
description and theory
description or theory
theory and theory and description and theory
description or theory
theory and description or
theory or description or theory and description

EUROPEAN BRIEF THERAPY ASSOCIATION

Publishing house and print: BoD – Books on Demand, Norderstedt

Cover design, typesetting, editing: Matthias Schwab

Photograph by Dave Hogan used by kind permission

www.ebta.eu – contact: peter.sundman@taitoba.fi

ISBN 978-37-519767-4-9

Knowledge is in the end
based on acknowledgement.

Ludwig Wittgenstein, On Certainty, §378.

CONTENTS

Foreword

The quest for a solution-focused practice theory started after Steve de Shazer's death with Gale Miller's and Mark McKergow's "bigger picture" meetings in 2008. These were meetings looking for similar ideas to those in the solution-focused tradition. Many similarities were found especially in philosophy. The meetings were engaging and liberating. "We could explain solution-focused practice in ways that did connect with what others have said. There was also something distinct and quite unique in this approach. Could we describe this more precisely and could we agree?"[1] That was something interesting to find out!

The *European Brief Therapy Association* (EBTA) established a group to define solution-focused practice and in 2010 the first "Practice Definition" was discussed by the board and, to our surprise, agreed on! Yes, there were some differences in emphasis, but with several possibilities included, no substantive disagreements remained.

The next milestone in the development of this theory was Janet Bavelas' and Harry Korman's plenary and workshop "Does SFBT have a Theory?" at EBTA's annual conference in 2014.[2] They had dug through Steve de Shazer's books and presented what they called the "postulates for a theory of

---

[1] Sundman, personal note from these meetings.

[2] Bavelas et al. (2014).

solution-focused brief therapy". So, even Steve de Shazer, although critical about explaining his and his colleagues work, had a theoretical foundation! – This encouraged us in the EBTA group to continue the quest in a more theoretical direction.

Two other interesting perspectives have been of major importance in our work.

Firstly, how to ground the ideas and goals within the solution-focused community. This is interesting, because the practice is open in the sense that no one has copyright to it. Grounding it with colleagues was a way to get a sense what the solution-focused community wants and accepts. As a consequence, the text we now propose, has been discussed in all EBTA conferences since and with many colleagues as well as with our trainees. We were also happy that other organisations and persons in recent years have presented their ideas about what solution-focused practice is.

The other interesting perspective is that the "Ockham's razor" principle of using the simplest principles has been a guiding principle by most of the solution-focused developers. Here we disembark from this tradition in presenting a more inclusive theory with several principles of practice, several ways of practicing SF. This makes SF somewhat less distinctive, but more usable in different contexts and styles.

Finally, a remark about contexts. Solution-focused work is practiced with good results in surprisingly different contexts.

The expansion continues to the extent that we decided to propose that this theory is applicable in many contexts. However, leaving the boundaries of solution-focused practice undefined, might be considered a weakness, as we assume they exist. Hence, this and other aspects need to be addressed in the future.

So, the quest will continue! And we invite all our readers to become part of this ongoing conversation.

July 2020,
EBTA Practice Definition Task-Group

Theory of Solution-Focused Practice

2020 Version, by

Peter Sundman

Matthias Schwab

Ferdinand Wolf

John Wheeler

Marie-Christine Cabié

Svea van der Hoorn

Rytis Pakrosnis

Kirsten Dierolf

Michael Hjerth

Introduction

This document is the result of a collaboration between a number of authors working as a *European Brief Therapy Association* (EBTA) task-group. The authors have exchanged versions of this paper over a number of years. Earlier versions have been offered to a variety of audiences – the EBTA Board, at conferences, and informally amongst colleagues in order to invite and include multiple perspectives on this contentious topic of a theory for solution-focused practice. The co-authors look forward to comments and feedback so that further spirals of evolution can continue.

Our aim in this document is to present a coherent theory of solution-focused practice for those who want to understand the rationale, together with a comprehensive description of solution-focused practice that can be used for training and developmental purposes.

Theory here is defined as a process theory[1] describing how the solution-focused practice is done, together with explanations of how and why the process is initiated, why it goes in a certain direction and who is responsible for it. The rationale

---

[1] Morris (2005). A process theory is a system of interconnected and interacting concepts, which attempts to explain and predict how something is happening rather than what it is.

and assumptions that the theory are based on and general predictions of the outcome are also described.

This document is also meant as a statement of what solution-focused practice, its preferred, supposed, ideal, choices and assumptions can be claimed to be.[2]

Solution-focused practice builds on the work of Milton Erickson (Erickson 1954a, 1954b), as popularised by Haley (1986), (client beliefs, individuality, capacity to change, personal choice, relationships, language, instructions, interaction), the work of the Mental Research Institute (Weakland et al. 1974), (interaction, behaviour, acting differently, frames of reference, reframing) and ideas from systemic therapy (for example Cecchin 1987, Minuchin 1974 & Selvini-Palazzoli et al. 1973), (cybernetics, communication, feedback, relations, networks, complexity). Theoretically, social constructivism, language philosophy, namely the work of Ludwig Wittgenstein, and Buddhist thinking have inspired the developers of the practice[3].

The practice is based on over thirty years of theoretical development, clinical practice, and empirical research by Insoo Kim Berg, Steve de Shazer and their colleagues and clients at the Milwaukee Brief Family Therapy Center in the early

---

[2] The solution-focused approach has been called "a rumour" by Gale Miller and Steve de Shazer (Miller & de Shazer 1998), because developers and trainers commonly only express what they think solution-focused thinking and practice is.

[3] Watzlawick (1980), de Shazer et al. (2006), Miller & McKergow (2012).

1980s. Solution-focused practice since is being developed by many professionals in many countries all over the world.

The main approach in the development has been inductive, actively searching for logical arguments in the clinical practice that indicate support for certain practices, conclusions and theoretical generalizations.[4] The micro-analysis research by Janet Bavelas and her team has added an abductive approach (Lipton 2001) – pattern-seeking that oscillates between what takes place in the lived world between clients and practitioners and the world of abstract ideas.

Solution-focused practice is open for anyone to develop further, which makes the question of what it is unclear – and is a further reason for making this theory. Our effort has been to collect and fit together many well argued and founded ideas that logically fit into a coherent framework. This work began in 2007 with a series of meetings investigating the connections between solution-focused ideas and other ideas in philosophy, sociology, psychology and related fields. In 2010 EBTA founded a task group to formulate a *Practice Definition*, which was adopted by EBTA in 2012 and revised in 2013. The task-group has continued its work hosting open discussions at conferences, informal discussions with colleagues and collecting published data.[5] During these years

---

[4] Well documented arguments are for instance the concepts and use of exceptions, the miracle question and scales.

[5] Among others: Open Space discussions at the EBTA conferences (2015 - 2019), discussion at the SFT-List (2017).

others have also introduced related frameworks, like the *Solution Focused Therapy Treatment Manual for Working with Individuals* by the SFBTA, *Clues 1.1 and 1.2* (list of SF signs in action) by SFCT and the UKASFP *Accreditable Practice and Accreditable Practitioners* (2015), together with several articles showing the general interest in defining the solution-focused approach.[6]

We are aware of the reservations regarding the theory that we propose here.[7] There has, however, always been rigorous reasoning grounding solution-focused practice.[8] The first framework similar to this was already written in 1996.[9] Making this reasoning explicit, will, we believe, be helpful for the further development of the practice. The theory shows itself in the conceptual assumptions, in the notions and pre-suppositions we ascribe to, and within the descriptions of the practice we use.

Solution-focused practice was initially developed in a thera-peutic context. A characteristic is that it evolved in the con-text of family therapy as well as individual therapy. Thus,

---

[6] For instance Froerer & Connie (2016), McKergow (2016) or Korman (2017).

[7] For example, Steve de Shazer wrote in *Words* were *originally magic*: "I de-cided that my only recourse was to follow Wittgenstein's advice (1958) and renounce all Theory"(de Shazer, 1994, p.32) and in the well-known interview with Michael Hoyt he said: "Don't let the theory get in the way. Theories will blind you." (Hoyt, 2001, p.29).

[8] The first theoretical reasoning was published in 1974 (Weakland et al. 1974).

[9] Berg & De Jong (1996).

right from the start, solution-focused practice needed to stretch itself and be sufficiently robust and flexible to be relevant and appropriate when working with both individuals and groups. From the 1980's, it has spread into different fields of work such as coaching, education, group work, leadership, organizational development and consulting. This theory is meant to be applicable in all the different areas of solution-focused work, though examples and descriptions might show bias to the therapeutic context, because of the authors' practice background and the original development in this context. Further discussion and analysis will probably show where this theory requires further development in order to fit well. In the SF world, theory is only as useful as it is pragmatic. It should enable research, support practitioners and enhance the quality of services to clients.

We use the name "solution-focused practice" as the name of this theory to acknowledge both the originators and other newer developers inside and outside of the therapeutic context. Some readers may be familiar with the term "solution-focused brief therapy" (SFBT) from the therapeutic context. We acknowledge this name as being part of the history of the form of practice that this document explores and expands on. Others in the organizational field use the term "SF Practice" when describing what we here call *solution-focused practice*.

The words "client" and "clients" are here used as a collective name for the person or persons, who seek partnering and support in their change journeys. All clients belong to many groups, like a couple, family or a team with their own unique values, language, goals and behaviour. It is common practice to take these groups into account and involve them and persons from them in the change process, because it opens up possibilities for using their patterns of interaction, their different points of view and alternatives, to do behavioural experiments and to evaluate multiple consequences of change.[10]

The client's change is thus a change also for these groups. For instance, when individual staff members change, their department changes and the company changes to some extent. Sometimes what starts as one person's change ends with a large-scale change. Sometimes the organizational group or the specific setting sets requirements for the person's change.

These specific group issues are mostly implicitly indicated in the text. A question to the client can then be a question inviting individual responses from many persons in the group, or a reply that represents the group as a whole. SF practice honours the individual within the interactional web, without privileging the individual over the collective.

The theory has three interrelated parts. It starts with describing the context of solution-focused practice. Secondly, the conceptual thinking and the reasons for the basic model of solution-focused practice, together with the main ethical

---

[10] de Shazer (1991).

choices and assumptions, are presented. Finally, characteristic elements and key topics in solution-focused conversations are highlighted in a description of the change process. The parts offered below overlap and relate to each other. All have something unique about them. Practice cannot, for example, be fully described or explained, as language doesn't capture everything. Each moment in life is unique and different from what concepts can cover. Our thinking requires intuitions, but on the other hand, "intuitions without concepts are blind"[11].

Like the original solution-focused developers, we want to keep the focus on what is happening in practice and not get distracted or become rarefied by the explanations, which can easily happen among professionals. All the same, we want to make some basic concepts clear in order to explain the reasons for what is done in solution-focused practice.

Both explanation and description can be seen as mutually inter-dependent conceptual frames or surfaces of a space that is created by practice.

Our actions and how we live our daily lives get described and explained from different sides and angles. However, our acting may, and by means of creativity will, go beyond theory as well as description in many ways. This will not be seen in terms of theory or description unless we expand our theory or description. Our stance is thus that practice is foundation-

---

[11] Kant (1914, p.75).

al to its reflection in the oscillation between describing and explaining what people do.

I. Practice: Being in context

Practice is something no one can do away with. Humans can stop thinking and reflecting or even be fully unaware of their doings, but they cannot stop practice. Furthermore, all forms of human practice inevitably are performed in some context. The concept "context" is here used as a way to differentiate different practices from each other. This section describes what is the context for solution-focused practice and what context is created by and within solution-focused practice.

All professional practices, solution-focused practice too, happen somewhere, at a particular time, and in direct or imagined relation to someone and something which is referred to as "being in context".

Contexts are social interactional situations that frame how people perceive, use, interpret language and act. "Feeling better" means something different expressed with a medical doctor compared to what it means with a spouse, for instance. The meaning of "feeling better" can also be negotiated and changed by referring to hopes for the future rather than past experiences. Words can be given to what has been inarticulable and change the meaning of a context, like "feeling better, because you take me seriously, which in fact is the issue".[12]

People also create and change their contexts. So, what is relevant in a coaching session is thus different from what is relevant in a therapy session.

Contexts also define relationships and roles. For example, in a consulting room, the relationship between two people is complementary. A client seeking help can perceive a therapist as being in the superior position.[13] The same people meeting during a party will not have the same type of relationship, although the context of their therapeutic relationship could still affect their interactions at the party. Furthermore, depending on the context, people behave differently. Caregivers often experience this when they accompany a group of patients outdoors to restaurants, the patients' behaviour is very different from that in the care unit.

These contexts of social interaction are conditional to individual reflections and vice versa.[14] This means that meaning cannot be separated from the context in which words and actions are used and interpreted. In addition, any word used refers to other words and actions in other contexts used by other persons with other meanings. Contextual meaning also

---

[12] Miller & McKergow (2012).

[13] Clients as hiring customers can also perceive themselves as superior.

[14] Lauth (1989).

involves a more general orientation to (or a sense of) what is at issue in the interaction and its implications for the past and future.[15] Categorizing someone, for example, as a "mother" or "schizophrenic", ascribes meaning to the person and the context. This ascription of meaning is more and in most cases something different than giving a thing a name tag. It involves a complex process and history of intentions, values, experiences, and social interactions.

The specific context in which solution-focused work originally evolved was the psychotherapeutic practice context, which is often defined as "talking cure"[16]. The talk, the conversation, has been seen as a vehicle for change and hence has been a major area of interest, reflection and research. In this context, someone who experiences problems in their life seeks confidential[17] help from a trained practitioner. Sometimes practitioners can observe the context where the client wants the change, for instance when they meet a whole family or work group.

What clients and practitioners do together is usually a temporary addition to the clients' life and the clients use the

---

[15] Miller (2008).

[16] de Shazer et al. (2007). "Talking Cure" was first introduced in 1895 by Joseph Breuer and Sigmund Freud in *Studien über Hysterie*.

[17] Confidentiality has, for example, played an important role in the definition of psychotherapy. Meaning that the therapist has to ensure that outsiders don't get to know what has been said in the therapy room.

therapeutic experiences as support for their change.[18]

Dealing with problems in this context usually leads to talk about the negative consequences of them: what is wrong, what causes the problems and what obstacles to overcome. We will here show that solution-focused practice creates another kind of context, often called "solution-building"[19]. Solution-focused practice emphasizes clients' competencies, agency and past successes. It focuses on interactions around how clients can use their resources and strengths to make the best possible changes for a better life. This theory is therefore a theory of how change in solution-focused practice happens and how it supports clients to implement those changes in their lives.[20]

As solution-focused practice spread into different fields of work such as coaching, education, group work, leadership, organizational development and consulting, words, the language and actions of the solution-focused practice has and will change to some degree. In coaching, for instance, there might not be a need for help with troubles, rather a will to develop further and achieve more goals. The full scope of contexts, where solution-focused practice is usable and can contribute value is still emerging.

---

[18] Usually the clients use their therapeutic experience by themselves in their everyday life.

[19] For instance DeJong & Berg (2012); Miller & McKergow (2012).

[20] Bavelas, J., Korman, H., DeJong, P., Smock, S. (2016).

A general definition of the solution-focused practice in these different practice contexts is: Clients get support for the change they hope for from a practitioner based on the clients' resources, skills, strengths, future hopes and interaction in their environment. For the clients it means formulating and applying new orientations to self, others and the future.[21] This is thus a theory of how to support a client's change.[22]

Practice, as indicated above, also implies more than the interaction described here. Even the most intimate conversations in "talking cures" involve interaction related to personal, social, legal, political, cultural and religious (to name a few) issues. No description or explanation can ever do complete justice to life. There is always more to it. As practice creates the open space of life, the context of ascribed meanings, and is an ongoing interrelated process, it will inevitably be changing and evolving across space and time.

We will in the next sections describe the solution-focused practice, its focus of attention, use and reasons for choosing this practice, instead of other ways of being in context.

---

[21] See also Miller & McKergow (2012).

[22] Bavelas, J., Korman, H., DeJong, P., Smock, S. (2014).

II. Explanation: Why be solution-focused?

Some say that descriptions of solution-focused practice, continuous inductive development together with the growing empirical evidence that solution-focused treatments are efficient and effective[23], are enough of a reason to use solution-focused practice.[24] Solution-focused practice is however not grounded on descriptions alone, clinical results, social acceptance or personal style, but on rigorous reasoning and certain assumptions and values. Choosing the solution-focused practice therefore is based on both theoretical reasons and certain ethical choices.

This section will explore the reasoning in respect of three aspects of solution-focused practice as an activity of helping clients to change: a) the meaning of their situation, b) their self-perception and direction and c) everyday actions accordingly. The chapter ends with a summary of the main assumptions, values and beliefs of solution-focused practice.

---

[23] Macdonald (2017).

[24] de Shazer (2006).

Changing meaning

Solution-focused practice is partly a philosophical endeavour of talking about in what way it makes sense for the clients to conceptualize their experiences and how this may help to promote experiences of "feeling better" or "understanding better" – common requests that clients bring as their desired outcome when they start work with a practitioner. The solution-focused stance argues that language philosophy[25] makes a strong case for the practice of being helpful to other people, because the use of language is a fundamental element of conversation. Understanding and explaining the meaning of meaning, therefore, is of major importance. This includes making sense of perceptions, feelings, thoughts and intentions.

Meaningful sentences make a conceptual map of the world

Ludwig Wittgenstein and social constructionist philosophy is an important source of inspiration in conceptualizing the re-

---

[25] This term here is meant to include a variety of philosophical endeavours (i.e. transcendental philosophy (for example: Lütterfelds: Fichte and Wittgenstein, 1989), social constructivism (for example: Hacking: The Social Construction of What?, 1999) or enactivism (for example: Hutto & Myin: Radicalizing Enactivism, 2012) that are connected with core arguments of Wittgenstein's thinking, without going into details. In this sense we take fundamental arguments from "language philosophy" that explain some theoretical implications of the solution-focused stand.

lation of language and what we call "reality"[26]. Wittgenstein claimed that the limits of our language determine the limits of our world, and that world and life are one.[27] Language is thus not just a collection of words. It is the expression of a form of life.[28] What commonly are called facts are not things, but they are verbal expressions of meaningful sentences. These facts show a picture of reality and together are a model of the world. Words and sentences do not however have a fixed sense or meaning. They get their meaning from the context of life events and they are used in relation to other persons. So, what one says makes sense because of one's daily acting.[29] Thus – as Wittgenstein put it – the world of the happy is quite another than that of the unhappy.[30]

Human experience is not simply given, but more like a conceptual map or network where sense and meaning varies according to when, where, and how one relates to others.[31] Words, sentences, thoughts, and actions have varying refer-

---

[26] Miller & McKergow 2012.

[27] Wittgenstein: Tractatus logico-philosophicus, 5.6 and 5.621.

[28] Wittgenstein: Philosophical Investigations.

[29] Wittgenstein: On Certainty, § 229.

[30] Wittgenstein: Tractatus logico-philosophicus, 6.43.

[31] When talking of language or experience as a model or map of the world created from a network of meaningful signs, we have to be aware that there is no "world" behind them, we can know of, as knowing is only within these conceptual frames. However, there might be necessary concepts and one might be the concept of a "world" or "thing-in-itself" to use a Kantian term.

ences, denotations, connotations, implications, ambiguities, and contradictions.[32]

In this sense, the partly philosophical endeavour of solution-focused practice can be understood as a joint activity of world changing.[33]

The world is uncertain

Two implications of this understanding of meaning as a result of social interaction are to be mentioned. They also point to the next sections. The first implication is about how social interactions define rules. Because there are infinite ways to build sentences or even invent new words, thoughts and actions, it looks as if there are no possible foundations of language games and meaning.[34] Radical constructivists do indeed claim this to be the case, while others point to the inherent self-contradiction of such claims.[35] If there were no foundation of meaning, how would there be meaning at all?

---

[32] The different terms we used here (models, maps, networks) indicate different aspects of meaning. One aspect is that of representation, abstraction and highlighting certain aspects when thinking of language as a model or map. Another aspect is that of interdependency, interwoven relations and linking in or referring to other aspects when thinking of a network of meanings and language games.

[33] Another metaphor for this activity is to say that the conversation "stretches the world of the client" (McKergow, 2020).

[34] Wittgenstein: Philosophical Investigations.

[35] von Foerster & Pörksen (2002).

This question touches on the fundamental question of certainty and truth, and we humble ourselves to an observation in line with Wittgenstein. The picture of reality people have varies in extremes across cultures and times, and one has to be very careful with judging and comparing the incomparable. But, any form of life with all possible differences rests upon judgements that can be imagined as hinges around which the variable system of meaning rotates. Any form of life, and any meaningful conceptual network, rest upon judgements, which cannot be reasonably doubted within this form of life. Wittgenstein calls these fundamental sentences "hinges of our view of the world". We do not explicitly learn these sentences, but we may discover them like an axis of rotation that is defined by the movement around it.[36] Whether one agrees with what transcendental philosophers described as universal a priori concepts of knowledge[37] or not, the important point is that these fundamental judgements are not a matter of empirical investigations. Our life shows, for example, our certainty that there is no plug at the bottom of the sea, although no one ever bothered to find any empirical evidence for it. Even more, this applies to our experience in general. We, for example, cannot do without the concept of causality when saying: "I see the sea". There is, of course, no need to try to make these fundamental judge-

---

[36] Wittgenstein: On Certainty, §152.

[37] This is the purpose of Kant in the *Critique of Pure Reason* or of Fichte in his *Science of Knowledge*.

ments of our meaningful view of life explicit. In general, they just show up, just like life itself.[38]

Support to pursue a purpose

When people experience stuckness in relation to a problem, or want to change, and do not find a way to go about creating this change, or experience failed attempts at change, they usually expresses the problematic experience as being stuck, uncertain, in discomfort, troubled, confused with themselves, others and/or the current life situation or not able to reach their goals. Feeling hopeless and out of control is common. This takes us to the second implication. When people seek help, it implies that they experience some kind of hindrance in pursuing a purpose. Something that *should* be, or *could* be, is not. The purpose of actions, hopes and intentions are called values.[39] The client's values at stake in any conversation are the backbone of the conversation. They are not necessarily talked about, but solution-focused practitioners should be aware of them and as described later, respect people's choice of them. This also means that people have the capacity to determine their actions in relation to others and the world.

This line of reasoning has some important theoretical consequences that are liked to the reasons, why solution-focused practice is chosen. In the wake of Wittgenstein's thinking,

---

[38] Wittgenstein: On Certainty, § 559.

[39] Raz (2017).

solution-focused practitioners make the claim that there is no reasonable scientific way of explaining meaning by causal chains. It is not that the causal nexus is taken for a random fantasy, but it just cannot explain semantic relations. Thus, solution-focused practitioners do not understand the interacting persons and the exchange of meaning as determined by causal forces, be it the physical law, social or economic power structures, brains, genes, or other things. There is no doubt that it makes sense to speak of them, but they do not determine the meaning of the words and any meaningful conversation either.

The second argument from language philosophy that solution-focused practitioners take seriously is that personal perceptions, thoughts, beliefs, motives, values, states, scripts or any "inner entity or state" that we think determines our actions does not alone determine the meaning of the words we use and the actions we take, although most of us think they do. Instead, solution-focused practitioners rely on what might be called "creative interaction", where meaning is created in life events between people and this is the basis for solution-focused change.

This of course does not mean that such personal thoughts are irrelevant, but they do not have the exclusive controlling quality sometimes ascribed to them.

Change as new meaning in everyday life

Meaning, in line of this argument, shows in the way people live their lives, how they connect to other people and handle life's events and situations. Therefore, solution-focused practitioners pay attention to the detailed descriptions of people's daily life to discover and create meaningful sentences and actions that allow the person to get what they think is good and useful for them and to go about with whatever made them seek professional help.[40] The focus of the conversation is on the interaction between people. First, *in-between* the practitioner and the client, second, *in-between* the clients and significant other persons in their lifes, that will experience future behaviour. Quite often significant others and changes in the environment significantly contribute to the change, because the meaning *in-between* persons is necessarily a joint venture. Talk about forgotten, hidden, new or not yet considered utilizations of the words we use sets in motion a process of co-construction by persons in which altered or new meanings are generated.[41] This is another important part of the solution-focused practice.

---

[40] Some elaboration and case examples can be found in: McKergow & Korman (2008) and Iveson & McKergow (2016).

[41] McGee, Del Vento, & Bavelas (2005).

Changing self-perception and direction

Another aspect of solution-focused practice is to address clients' requests to make changes in their lives. These changes can be about changing perception of self and their world, orient themselves, expanding possibilities, adapt to limitations, solve problems and/or tackle challenges . This is often expressed as: "What can or should I do?" - "How can I change this?" - "How can I get this?" From this perspective solution-focused practice is a social practice of helping the client to become more satisfied with themselves and with their responses to their life situation. In this respect solution-focused practice is a client-centric practice[42] that takes clients' experiences, worldview and values as the basis for the help.

The solution-focused assumption is that everyone is *per se* capable of living a meaningful life, and of having done so already, even if they think or feel stuck at some point.[43] People have also overcome past difficulties. Furthermore, they can adapt to their life circumstances and will manage to get along. They have a purpose in life, even if they may not be

---

[42] More about this for instance here: http://journeys.getsynap.com/the-difference-in-being-customer-centric-vs.-customer-focused. Also similarities with Rogers (1951).

[43] Erickson (1980).

32

able to describe it in a coherent narrative.[44] Therefore, they are resourceful, competent and resilient. In other words, people have agency, and in this sense, they are the experts of their own life. Regarding clients' agency in their lives, practitioners cannot know where clients will choose to go and, so, solution-focused practitioners do not claim to know.[45] Helping clients to see their agency, competence, and resources in the light of their purpose of life, is considered a respectful, empowering, and effective way to enable them to go on with their lives and overcome whatever made them seek support. This is the solution-focused concept of human beings (persons).[46]

Building with competence and resilience

Given that people have already constructed their world, and even though it might not be with sense and meaningfulness all the time, it is still meaningful to some extent and in some contexts. Therefore, there is always something to build on, and even in seemingly desperate situations people can come up with amazing coping skills, resources and resilience. Thus, the practitioner calls the clients to look for their power and agency in life by inviting descriptions of these particular nominalizations (skills, strength, resources, etc.) in fluid,

---

[44] Re-establishing the purpose can be challenging in some life situations like, in loss of loved ones.

[45] This is commonly called "not-knowing" (Anderson & Goolishian 1992).

[46] In German "Menschenbild".

verbal forms. Consequently, solution-focused practitioners will usually not ask questions on how and why the situation became that desperate, nor collect details of all the hardships.[47] Instead the solution-focused practitioner asks about how the client is contributing to keeping things steady rather than things getting worse.

In order to talk about how clients can go on with their sense and meaning, it is not necessary to fully understand or analyze their view of the world (all sentences and hinges), but it is enough to establish a workable fit that allows the client to go on with his life. This implies that whatever the client wants to share is enough to work with. Solution-focused practitioners do not think that there has to be an agreed upon and unified way of life and they value the diversity of unique solutions by each client.

As respect and support of the client's purpose and view of the world has been chosen as the bottom line of the solution-focused practice, clients are trusted to know what changes they want and trusted to collaborate as well as possible in making the change happen.[48] This means that solution-focused practitioners base their relation with the client on the premise of respect for the client's beliefs, autonomy, safety, and needs. It also means that practitioners strive to

---

[47] McKergow & Korman (2008).

[48] For instance, the Solution-focused treatment manual (2013).

minimize their involvement in the client's life.[49] This is done to enable people to empower themselves to live a meaningful life according to their own values. Empowerment is understood as inviting clients to become aware of their power and agency in taking control of the meaningful change they seek. It is mostly personal empowerment, to some extent interpersonal empowerment in relation to significant others, and sometimes socio-political empowerment, to access resources and questioning commonly held truths.[50] From this choice it follows that solution-focused practice is not defining a norm according to a numeric normal of statistical descriptions. The concept of "normal" is actually empty and there is always only deviance and change.[51] Normality in mental health and life is a cultural, ideological and political choice.[52] This choice should not be mistaken for a normative value of how life or persons should be. Strengthening the client's competences requires that the practitioner creates a safe and comfortable interactional space, where clients can express their thoughts well and in which the practitioner is open, curious, respectful, appreciative and genuine towards them. This also requires that the practitioner builds on hope, positive emotions, virtues, caring, love, compassion, gratitude, and

---

[49] These ethical choices are described in more detail in the EBTA code of ethics (2015).

[50] Rappaport et al. (1984).

[51] de Shazer (1994, p107).

[52] Berger, Luckmann, Zifonum (2002).

sympathy for the clients and their environment. It is assumed that this all helps clients to cope with current hardships, broadens the scope of attention, recognise signs of change and inspires them to generate change, creating more positive emotions that further evoke skills for change.[53]

Solution-focused practitioners use the client's capacity to construct and build on their and others' useful experiences, coping strategies, problem solving abilities, learning experiences, resilience, resources, strengths, skills, talents and successes. The practitioner listens carefully to elicit and amplify what might be helpful in all phases of the conversation and change process. Some resources are implicit. Solutions are, for instance, often implied in problem descriptions. Problems can be described as unfulfilled hopes. Talking about best hopes implies that they can be achieved. Talking about past changes implies that more of them are possible. Once the clients are aware of their power to influence, the meaning of actions and agency, there can be less emphasis on failings, inabilities, motives, conflicts, obstacles and problems.[54]

In some situations, clients might need alternatives to counterproductive or harmful behaviour, interaction, cognitions

---

[53] Fredrickson (2013), Shick (2017).

[54] There is a lot of ambiguity associated with "empowerment". Furthermore, how much or with which means practitioners support their client's empowerment has not for instance been discussed much among solution-focused practitioners. A group called *The Solution-Focused Collective* started in 2018 a movement to address social change to avoid public issues to be translated to personal troubles (The Solution-Focused Collective, 2019).

and feelings. In these situations, clients are helped to do something different within their repertoire and their values and frame of reference. The reasoning behind such interactions seems strikingly simple: if you are unhappy with what you did so far, try something else. Yet, it is not self-evident to refrain from giving advice and taking an expert position of where the client could or should be.[55]

Towards the best possible change

To support clients' competence even further, solution-focused practice introduces the idea of the best possible change. A best possible change can be the client's vision, a miracle scenario, best hopes from the conversation, succeeding perfectly or another of their ideals. Describing the best possible change helps the clients to make sense, strengthens their competencies, and helps them to find meaningfulness for themselves.[56] Sometimes the client's miracle actually happen and clients' lives change drastically for the better.

As indicated earlier, the conversation is treated as an intersubjective endeavour.[57] Both parties collaborate together and contribute to the result. Inevitably practitioners therefore influences the client in many ways, particularly through the

---

[55] This principle is debated among practitioners. Some use this MRI originated principle alongside the 'do more of what works' principle. Others are careful not to suggest any of their own ideas to their clients (George 2010).

[56] de Shazer et al. (2006).

[57] Peräkylä et al. (2008).

assumptions they use in their conversational tools. It is important that practitioners are aware of the personal agenda they implicitly or directly contribute to the conversation.

Solution-focused practitioners are aware of the fact that being helpful in a solution-focused spirit is a specific kind of agenda as well.

So, solution-focused practitioners, on the one hand, intentionally influence the general direction of the conversation in promoting solution talk. In doing this, solution-focused practitioners take responsibility for their intents and choices during the conversation. The emphasis to build on existing meaning and competency, and looking for hopes and the best possible future, is already an important choice in respect to the client's agency, as it usually leads to relatively fewer conversations and therefore arguably limits dependency on practitioners.[58] By using the key solution-focused assumptions, and the specific solution-focused emphasis on conversational tools, they offer their view of the world as a possible way for the client to choose to look.

On the other hand, practitioners stay as much as possible within the world of the client to limit their influence. In a way, they visit the clients's world and use their observations for the clients to make more sense, promote change, create meaning and meaningfulness and act towards what is mea-

---

[58] Macdonald, (2017).

ningful to them, to be able to proceed in life and end the conversation with the professional practitioner.

And some professional support

The ethical choices described above do not prohibit practitioners from reflecting, interpreting or giving advice, if the client asks for it and if the situation calls for it.[59] To do otherwise could be dangerous for the client, and a dereliction of the duty of care on the part of the practitioner. Interpretations and advice are given in a way that fits the client's view of the world and as one possibility of many. Practitioners are aware that conflicting values are common amongst people. The practitioner helps the client to consider and solve such conflicts, for example, helping clients to balance between their perspective and the need for them to respect the law, social norms and the well-being of others.

Changing actions

Finally, because of the trust in the capability of the client to pursue a meaningful life, solution-focused practice is future oriented and offers practical support that helps the clients to act and achieve their ends. This also exposes the extent to

---

[59] SF practitioners have different opinions about this. From discussions with colleagues we have noticed that some say they avoid and some say they don't give any advice.

which the client's sense is sensible, i.e. contributes to a more meaningful life.

Change is sensible when the consequences are as intended

Everything in the conversation aims at supporting the client's meaningful acting to make their values happen in the future. Changes become meaningful when the consequences are as intended and can be observed in the future. Solution-focused practice builds upon the future aspect of the client's intention to achieve something of value. The better and the more detailed the descriptions of how one will do this in the future are, the better one knows what to do, and the easier it will be to do it.[60] Thus, solution-focused practice supports and strengthens people's agency.[61]

Again, there is a very simple reason for this hope and value driven future orientation: only what has not yet happened can be changed, therefore any change is yet to come.

Of course, one can always change the way one thinks about the *meaning* of what has already happened. Such changes can change life dramatically. Still, this change will only happen from now onwards and into the future.

---

[60] Positive psychology research on meaningfulness, well-being, prosperity and happiness indicate that meaningfulness is associated with purpose and *eudaimonia*, being part of something more than oneself (Seligman, 2011).

[61] Walter & Peller (1992), Shennan (2016).

Reflected and evaluated

A future orientation connects with the two previous solution-focused aspects of change. First, the practitioner helps the client to define the change and then to decide the meaningfulness of the consequences and anything that might be different, when the intended change would be realized. This relates the change to the client's values and meaning of life. The practitioner therefore talks with the client after the actions have been taken, whether the change related actions in the client's view have meaningful consequences. If not, the practitioner repeats the change process with the client to modify some aspect of it. When clients no longer feel stuck and express confidence that they know how to continue with their life, the co-construction can end. Clients are welcome to return if and when they deem it appropriate. In solution-focused practice it is common for clients to decide how many sessions and at what intervals. The idea of thinking negatively about clients for example as "revolving door" or "repeat" clients is not a part of solution-focused practice. At the same time solution-focused practitioners see themselves as partners in a co-construction process where the client signals when that partnership can be brought to a close.

Over 30 years of solution-focused practice has shown that clients can and do make these sorts of changes when offered these co-created conversational contexts.[62]

---

[62] Macdonald (2017). A list of research on client's experiences of solution-focused practice could be a useful addition.

The main assumptions, values and beliefs

What are the core assumptions, beliefs and values about people and change in solution-focused practice?

There are many lists of assumptions, values and beliefs.[63] Here we will make a short summary of the most important ones used in this theory together with what view of the world they portray and what ideology they indicate.[64]

Language is the key element in solution-focused practice, because language provides the means for people to make sense of their experiences. Interaction with others gives words and sentences their meaning. These described interactions make a conceptual map with which they orient and express themselves. Therefore exploring the client's map with the client's words is one of the practitioner's most important tasks to help both the client and the practitioner to focus their attention on what the client wants and to support the client's change.

Solution-focused practice is based on the belief that people are enactive: They discover the world by exploring it and making sense of it by observing, thinking, feeling, intuiting. People can choose and are able to live a meaningful life according to their own standards. They are capable of noticing,

---

[63] For instance Wheeler & Vinnicombe (2011), Wells (2018).

[64] These are tentative thoughts at this point, as it is, as far as we know, done for the first time.

judging and defining useful differences and changes. People are also seen as experienced in coping with difficult situations and in overcoming these situations.

People are assumed to want to be respected as enactive and to live a meaningful life according to their own terms, to be seen in their competences, their desires, their uniqueness and their awareness of doing meaningful things.[65] These unique life experiences of the clients' are regarded as their special expertise.

Solution-focused practice has taken the client's life experiences as the basis for the collaboration. It is designed to support people in their expertise.

The practitioner then looks for the person's hopes for the future, abilities, creativity and attempts to cope with and deal with the situation they want to change. This focus on the client's desired future is a choice based on clinical experience.[66] Also research indicates that focusing on positive aspects of life, on possibilities, a better future are powerful ways to empower people.[67]

At the same time solution-focused practice assumes that change happens in the client's social context. Meaning is made and shared with others. The preferred change gets its

---

[65] For support of this assumption, see for instance Deci & Ryan (2000).

[66] Gingerich & Eisengart (2004).

[67] Positive psychology research like Fredriksson (2015).

meaning and sense in actions with others. Therefore many questions are about preferred changes in the relationships and the environment at hand. The emphasis is both to empower the client, to support negotiations with others and to support adaptation to the circumstances. The basic assumption is that people are creating a meaningful life in mutual interaction.

Solution-focused practice assumes that people's pictures are different and don't always fit together. Although some clients' preferred change at face value sometimes doesn't seem to fit others, a more detailed exploration about different possibilities nevertheless mostly leads to reasonable agreement.

How about conflicts? Some conflicts are misunderstandings that are resolved as they are talked about. In others practitioners might offer mediation.[68]

How do people develop these abilities? – Solution-focused practice doesn't have a theory of development of its own. Instead, when needed for the change at hand, it uses the theories individual clients find useful. Sometimes the practitioner, knowing the client's contextual map, can offer a suitable theory. Several theories from social psychology, discursive psychology and systems theory fit well with a solution-focused practice.

---

[68] For instance de Shazer et al. (2007).

Why do people experience problems despite their expertise? – The world as an infinite number of contextual maps with varied meaning is a complex world where anyone gets lost from time to time, offers a general explanation. Sometimes trying to use the wrong map (more of what doesn't work) seems to be a common attempt in difficulties.[69]

As shown in the chapter "Changing Meaning", solution-focused practice doesn't need to conceptualize why or how problems occur. Instead it uses the client's personal experiences and maps and the concepts that evolve in the practice interaction. This is the reality at hand.

As a consequence of regarding reality as a complex world with varied meaning, the future is negotiable and changeable. The assumption is that change occurs all the time and can be made in many ways. It can for instance be sudden, slow, shifting, permanent, gradient, surprising, evident, planned, creative, difficult, simple, or even impossible. Quite often small changes and differences lead to big changes[70]. Therefore most practitioners organize their support adjusted to specific situations, with step by step evaluation and reorientated when needed.[71]

---

[69] Watzlawick (1988).

[70] Often called "the ripple effect" and sometimes referred to as "the butterfly effect".

[71] Solution-focused practice is often labeled as "brief", because the preferred changes often happen in shorter time than in traditional 20th century therapeutic practice.

These beliefs, values and choices show that solution-focused practice values uniqueness, tolerance, pluralism and empowerment as core values.

III. Description: What makes practice solution-focused?

This description of practice is a simplified account of what actually happens in practice, in order to show how the explanatory concepts are used in practice. Here, we ask: What makes practice solution-focused? Like a professional conceptual map, this description highlights or omits features of the space of action that are specific to solution-focused practice. In this way the descriptive map helps differentiate Solution-focused practice from other kinds of "talking cures", "coaching models", "educational syllabuses", or "approaches".[72]

Solution-focused practice may look like a superficial conversation without any exchange on "deep or hidden causes, explanations and complex psychopathological mechanisms at work".[73] It is however a very focused co-constructive conver-

---

[72] Thus, the famous quote "The map is not the territory", by Alfred Korzybski coined at the meeting of the American Association for the Advancement of Science in 1931 became important for many solution-focused practitioners.

[73] Superficial and not addressing the real, underpinning problems has been the main critique against the solution-focused practice (de Shazer (1988)).

sation in which the practitioners concentrates on the moment at hand and the client's presence. They focus on the actual interchange of words and actions between them. They respond from moment to moment on what the client did and said before. They deliberately keep, elicit, amplify or add on specific solution-focused topics (outlined below) based on what they hear from the client and what seems to enable a joint co-construction towards the client's desired change. They carefully ground each speech turn to collaborate with the client towards a coherent mutually agreed description of the issue at hand. These continuous and often overlapping sequences are the building blocks of the co-construction in the conversation that accumulates a shared meaning.[74]

As solution-focused practice operates within the realm of the client's world, which means listening for and building on expressions of competence, empowerment and agency as well as the client's hopes, ideas and plans for the future, the practitioner avoids orders, like advice, suggestions, interpretations and requests from outside, except when clients ask for them

---

[74] Grounding seems to be a universal three step sequence of how shared understanding comes about. The speaker first presents new information. The addressees then respond that or how they have (not) understood the information. Finally, speakers confirm that the addressee has (not) understood them correctly. A new grounding sequence starts, if the addressees show that they don't understand or accept, or the speaker doesn't confirm or accept the answer until a shared meaning is negotiated. Sometimes the meaning remains unclear and weakens the results of the dialogue. Sometimes the personal meanings differ from the shared meaning Clark & Brennan (1991), Bavelas (2012), Bavelas et al. (2014).

and the practitioner has expertise to offer.[75] Sometimes advice, proposals and suggestions about new actions (doing something different) might be appropriate, for example in high risk situations and ethical conflicts. Even in these situations orders are nonetheless given as possibilities or options rather than as prescriptions from an expert.[76]

Key topics in solution-focused practice

Respect, engagement and positivity

Respect and engagement with the unique characteristics of the client form the stance of solution-focused practice.[77] The practitioner needs to be curious[78] and appreciative of what the client expresses. Clients usually engage in the conversation in a similar fashion, which leads to a relationship of equals in which the practitioner takes the leading responsibility for setting in motion a constructive growth oriented process and the client takes leading responsibility for offering the content relevant to their desired change. Respect and en-

---

[75] de Shazer (1984), McKergow & Korman (2009). Some experts do never give orders when working solution-focused. Instead they use another role, like official or parent, in rare occasions to give advice, for instance (Shennan 2017).

[76] Flatt & Curtis (2013).

[77] Froerer & Connie (2016). Shennan (2017) doubts that these are specific for SF practice.

[78] Gale Miller calls this "disciplined curiosity skill" (Miller, 2014).

gagement show up as validation, encouragement, compliments and being genuine together with non-verbal expressions like nodding, smiling and leaning forward. These usually create an optimistic atmosphere with expressed signs of hope, empathy, compassion, caring and humour.[79]

For example:

- *"I will do my best" - at the beginning of the support (to show caring).*

- *"Yes, and …" - when the client has described how an event went (to show appreciation).*

- *"What will you do then?" - after the client has described a step forward (to show curiosity and encouragement).*

- *"Well done!" - when the client has made progress (to show appreciation and validate).*

- *"When you are able to …" - building on what the client does already (to show hope and encouragement).*

- *"Yes, I can imagine that …" - when a client has told about difficulties the practitioner can imagine (to show empathy).*

---

[79] Shick (2017). We are aware that the specific meaning of these concepts are unclear. See for instance Hutto & Jurgens (2019) on enactive empathy.

- *"Wow, how did you do that?" - when a client tells about a success (to express respect, curiosity and positivity).*

Preservation and use of the client's language

The description of the client's world can be done using and interpreting language in many ways. Some clients use literal descriptive language. Some clients describe their life as a narrative that highlights the client's agency and life events.[80] Others use metaphors, which can offer alternative interpretations. Some use humour and creativity; they play with ambiguity, chance and contradictions and see things from different perspectives. Both metaphors and humour show how change doesn't need to be logical and can come from "outside of the box". When working with groups and teams the commonalities and differences in language offer significant opportunities to support groups or teams in developing shared meaning or at least respect around differences.

The practitioner connects with the client's use of language. This means using the client's core concepts and logic. If people use different types of language for the change at hand, the type that most clearly indicates change is a good choice to use. Within that language practitioners invite clients to find and use meaningful differences helpful for the desired change. They can, for example, use scales to assess the cur-

---

[80] Iveson & McKergow (2016).

rent situation in relation to the preferred change, the degree of progress and level of confidence to change.

For example:

- *"How would you describe your situation now?" - open questions to get the specific words and logic the client is using.*

- *"Can you give me an example of that?" - to get concrete descriptions from the clients' experiences when clients use abstract language.*

- *"When he says to you to work more, how do you want to respond?" - to make an interactional and sequential map of events.*

- *"So, what options do you have in this situation that you explained?" - to explore different perspectives.*

- *"What else tells you that things are going well?" - to enrich descriptions of the preferred change.*

- *"What would be a step in the right direction?" - to scale progress.*

- *"How far have you already come?" - to measure and assess progress.*

Alignment with and support for the client's desired change

The basic activity in solution-focused practice is to align with and support the client to make a desired change in perceptions, feelings, thoughts, intentions, choices and/or actions by facilitating talk that generates detailed descriptions of the desired change.[81] In this process, the practitioner talks with the client about anything that seems helpful for the client to make the desired change. Initially it can be about problems, unwanted habits, what's wrong and about limitations (what cannot be changed). The unwanted is treated as something that might be open to change.[82] There won't in general be much talk about why things went wrong and the practitioner does not apply any theory or model to explain causes for difficulties or problems.[83] This is often described as "evaluative responsiveness"[84], "helping from one step behind"[85], and "en-

---

[81] For case examples and a theory related discussion of descriptions in the therapy context see Iveson & McKergow (2016).

[82] In line with the saying: "Every problem is a frustrated dream". - Practitioners, situations and contexts differ in how much "problem talk" is useful in a conversation. Some practitioners actively make the transition to "solution building" right away, others listen more for openings in the dialogue.

[83] Some clients ask for theories and in some situations a theory is directly or indirectly available as common sense, for instance. In these situations, the theory or the theoretical concepts can be used as viable explanations.

[84] Kramer & Stiles (2015).

[85] Solution Focused Therapy Treatment Manual for Working with Individuals, 2nd version (2013).

visioning the clients' situation in relation to the change they hope for"[86]. It can be compared with driving a car forward while looking in the rear mirror from time to time to see what is coming from behind.[87]

The change can be anything purposeful, meaningful and sensible for the client and possible for the practitioner to support. It is usually constructed and agreed on from the client's description of the current life situation as something that is not yet present, but hopefully soon will be. The client's hopes, expectations, plans, visions and dreams are good starting points for the conversation of what to change. To envision the client's best hopes or a hypothetical day after the miracle of the problem no longer being a problem, is a powerful way to describe the desired change. It is usually co-constructed by eliciting one or more concrete and detailed descriptions of desirable differences in the life situation at hand, including significant others' perspectives as part of the description. In subsequent conversations the clients might revise what they want to change after considering the description of a better future and maybe after dealing with the consequences of the initial change. The change can also be described as part of the client's life narrative especially in significant life changes.[88]

---

[86] de Shazer et al. (2006).

[87] Feedback from the audience at the EBTA conference in Sofia 2018.

[88] Significant life-events like serious illness, accidents, death of a close person, but also ongoing suffering through social injustice, racism, or inequity.

This brings one of the most challenging aspects of solution-focused practice for new practitioners – how to respond when clients seem unable to describe a preferred future. It is easy then to slip into causal talk about why things are as they are, amplifying the stuckness. Solution-focused practitioners are aware that it's often in the small intricate details of people's lives that possibilities for change show up. Hence descriptions about the apparently banal and mundane everyday routines in people's lives are welcomed. Questions like "and what might be a sign that gives you a clue that change might be possible?" are seen as useful as questions that invite descriptions of clear and do-able change.

For example:

- *"How will you know that our meeting today was useful for you?" - to get a sense of the client's expectations and conveying belief in the support.*

- *"What kind of change are you looking for?" - as an invitation to the solution talk, when clients' have not yet talked about the change.*

- *"How are things when you have reached your goals?" - to get a description of the preferred change as a goal and implying that the goals will be reached.*

- *"What will be different when things are going very well?" - to get the critical aspects of the change and showing confidence in the client's ability to do well.*

- *"Suppose a miracle happens and the change actually happens...?"* - initiating a version of the classical *"miracle question"*, when the client has difficulties in describing the desired change.[89]

- *"How will others know that the change has happened?"* - to incorporate significant others' perspectives.

- *"What else is there?"* - to enrich the description.

Offering suitable support

Both the client and the practitioner have expectations on what could be supportive and what may not be. Talking about and agreeing on the support and its context focuses the conversation and makes it clear, meaningful and sensible for both. Solution-focused practice is built on the assumption that clients are capable of making sense for themselves when invited and called to do so. The practitioners therefore usually agree with the client's expectations of the support, as long as it is within their remit and ethical boundaries. Support is a co-constructed emergent property between client and practitioner in solution-focused practice, rather than an empathic overture offered from an expert position. It is a matter of (1) knowing what to do (2) being able to do it (3) actually doing it (4) sustaining it over time and (5) adapting to changing circumstances. A client might want, or need support in all of

89 Berg & Dolan (2001).

this and more in the beginning of the support. A statement from a client, such as *"Now I know what to do and confident I'll manage"* is a good indicator for ending the support.

For example:

- *"How can our meeting be of best help for you?" - to ask for specific ingredients of value for the client.*

- *"What should we have in mind in working together?"- when the client has experiences and maybe specific expectations of the relationship and for the support.*

- *"What should we concentrate on here today?" - to limit and focus the support on relevant aspects of change.*

- *"Where do you want to be on your scale in order for us to stop?" - to get a sense of when to end the support.*

- *"Is it ok to stop here?" - when the client implies ending and sometimes to initiate and end.*

Drawing on the client's competence and resource activation

Change is mostly achieved by drawing on the client's competence and activating resources, although these may be hidden or dormant at first.[90] Solution-focused practitioners use

---

[90] Gassmann & Grawe (2006).

the client's capacity to construct and build on their and others' useful experiences, coping strategies, problem solving abilities, learning experiences, resilience, resources, strengths, skills, talents and successes. The practitioner therefore listens for and initiates talk about them.[91] All basic solution-focused questions presuppose client resources and/or change. Competences are often connected to words like strengths, qualities, abilities, skills, knowledge, talent, coping, resilience, knowledge, know-how, expertise, experiences, learning, development, confidence, initiatives and wisdom. Some resources are personal: reasoning, determination, or willpower. Some are social, such as significant relationships, family, and other social support. Others can be physical, political, and economical. Talk about supportive emotions, what is going well, or what are healthy and happy parts of the client's life can also elicit useful resources for the change. Reflective talk about resources is often useful to help clients to become more aware of them. Questions and answers about client values can be of particular importance in conflicts and when the attempted acts for change don't work, because they indicate the client's preferred change.

For example:

- *"Did I hear correctly that you were able to …" - to surface possible resources.*

---

[91] We thank Plamen Panayotov for reminding us of the importance of letting the clients' ask their questions (Panayotov, 2020).

- *"When was this better or easier?"* - to suggest past success and progress.

- *"What has helped you before?"* - to use client experiences

- *"What skills can you use now with this?"* - to suggest that the client has useful skills.

- *"Which option do you want to use?"* - to use the client's expertise.

- *"Can your colleagues help you?"* - to activate social support.

- *"What keeps you going?"* or *"What drives you forward?"* - to use the client's values and determination.

Noticing and amplifying progress

Clients' competence usually shows up in signs of progress. Clients talk, for example, about better times and differences for the better. Surprisingly, quite often clients can give examples of the desired change already happening. The practitioner can make these visible using, for instance, evaluative "scales" that describe differences that make a difference for the client and then talk about what made this possible. Then, doing more of what works, is the solution-focused way to amplify progress.

Some progress is implicit, for instance when something exceptional[92] goes better than usual in the current situation, which can be regarded as potential progress. In very serious situations, and where the clients' context is one of limited influence over their situation, stopping the situation from getting worse and maintaining steadiness can be regarded as progress.

For example:

- *"What's better?" - beginning meeting with a progress report sets the stage for more.*

- *"Where are you now on your progress scale?" - to evaluate the present moment in relation to the change.*

- *"What does this that you have said mean to you?" - to get and use the client's evaluation.*

- *"What is your next step?" - suggests further change done by the client.*

- *"What do you need to do to get back on track?" - to support recovery after a set-back.*

---

[92] Exceptions in problematic situations have been major ingredients in solution-focused practice. Exceptions are here reformulated, in keeping with a trend to focus on the desired future from the onset without starting from the problems clients (in therapeutic contexts) usually experience when seeking support. See, for example, Iveson and McKergow (2016) for an account of how BRIEF have come to coin the term "instances" to denote occurrences of what the client wants.

- *"What else could you do?" - to get new ideas for doing something different.*

Thinking and doing differently

The notion of change implies that something needs to be different. Therefore, thinking differently (about meaning or choices) and/or doing something different (acting) are frequent topics in the conversation. New meaning often evolves from de- or recomposing facts and fictions of the conversation in a process of reframing.[93] When clients find themselves doing more of what doesn't work[94], it is useful to talk about what the client is doing that is preventing things from getting worse. This is often something that clients do not take credit for. Keeping themselves from slipping further goes unrecognized until clients and practitioners engage with the "not worse" question. Another option is exploring other acceptable[95] alternatives for the client that might serve the purpose of achieving the desired change. The alternatives can be logically derived or creatively generated. Other people

---

[93] Mattila (2001).

[94] Weakland et al. (1974).

[95] Any alternative needs to fit the client's purpose and intentions. What other approaches often call "resistance", from a solution-focused point of view, is a useful contribution of clients to indicate that there are better alternatives around that are worth to be explored or discovered.

who are able to see alternatives "out of the box" can be of great help.

For example:

- *"What would be something completely different?"* - *when nothing has helped the client so far.*

- *"What would really surprise others?"* - *in relationships that predict failure.*

- *"What if we look at this from this angle?"* - *when new perspectives could generate new actions.*

- *"Who could bring fresh ideas?"* - *to use the network's possibilities.*

- *"How about something like this ..."* - *to introduce something new to the client to consider.*

Testing the change – in life between sessions

Changes become meaningful when the consequences fit the intended purpose. Life is full of surprises and therefore putting the difference into practice in everyday life is an important test of whether or not the change makes sense and creates the improvements the client hopes for.

Sometimes it is useful to devise experiments or new habits[96] together with clients, to test ideas generated in the reality of the client's world. For clients facing challenging and risky situations, some form of confirmation of the safety, appropriateness, and do-ability of the change is also important. When the client has practised the change, like an experiment for example, a conversation whether the consequences were as intended, is similar to an exploration of the situation for change. If not, a new modified change process can be designed.[97]

For example:

- *"What tells you that things are getting better?" - to highlight positive change when the client talks about progress.*

- *"What is your next step to make progress?" - to support implementing the client's change.*

- *"How did your experiment go?" - when the client has tried out something new.*

- *"What more do you need?" - if the change isn't enough.*

---

[96] Isebaert (2015).

[97] Research done at the University of Salamanca (Prada & Beyebach, 2008) indicates that a better fit with the client's theory of change and/or a different kind of approach to change is significant in stuck cases (four meetings without desired change).

Tracking and evaluating the process

To keep the conversation supportive, empowering and focusing on the client's desired change, continuous evaluation is used at the beginning, during and at the end of the conversation.

During the conversation solution-focused practitioners use and listen to formulations with care to preserve and build on as much of the client's words as possible and to limit the influence of other ideas.[98] Also, what they omit is chosen with the client's perspective in mind. They introduce new words as supplements and answers to requests from the client to open up new possibilities. These are usually phrased as options or tentative questions. Practitioners are also ready to modify their formulations to fit the client's view. Clients presumably use formulations to make themselves understood and to direct the dialogue. They often contain what the client means, what is important for them, what they want and how to proceed. Solution-focused practitioners use client's formulations as much as possible.[99]

---

[98] Formulations are complex statements during the conversation, where the speakers make a summary of the gist of some part of the conversation. In doing this, they selectively preserve, omit, alter, and add something that contributes to the co-construction of a new version of that part. Formulations often contain interpretations, naming, reframing and reflections (Korman et al., 2013).

[99] Except if the proposed formulation is against the practitioner's values or common sense.

Reflections by those involved, particularly in the beginning and the end of conversations, are used to ground the interpretations and conclusions in the client's experience. These reflective elements in the conversation also prevent "solution forced"[100] attempts to rush into change before the meaning of the change appears sufficiently clear. Solution-focused practitioners usually reflect on competence, resources, and possibilities. The clients' reflections at the end of the conversation show their understanding at that point and is a good conclusion of the conversation.

For example:

- *"Do I understand you correctly that ..." - to check an interpretation.*

- *"Can what you said earlier be important?" - to check and remind of earlier topics.*

- *"What does this experience tell you?" - to evaluate something new.*

- *"How close have you come towards your goals?" - to measure client progress.*

- *"Are we maybe done for now?" - to check the client's sense of the process.*

---

[100] "Solution forced" is a risk and a mistaken way of applying SF (Nylund & Corsiglia, 1994).

- *"What is your conclusion for today?"* - *to reflect the present meeting.*

- *"What was useful today?"* - *to evaluate the present meeting.*

- *"I'm impressed by how well you did this...!"* - *to support the client's progress.*

IV. Conclusion

In conclusion, we hope our work together can make a helpful contribution to an understanding of solution-focused practice, and that this document can be a useful resource for trainers, practitioners and others interested in the development of the approach. This version is the product of our work together and contributions from many others who have offered perspectives directly to the authors and during workshops and presentations at conferences.

Accounts of the early days of solution-focused practice describe a culture of curiosity, sharing and debate which helped to bring the approach into being. We hope that our work will, in some way, nourish such a culture amongst the much larger number of people who now know and value the approach, and that such a culture will help to keep the approach alive and open to change. So, let us continue to discuss ideas, comments, and debate at EBTA conferences and elsewhere to ensure we do see further spirals of evolution.

Expanding the circle of ideas

The 2017 SF World conference provided us with a significant opportunity to share our work, test the document with colleagues and gather more ideas for the further development of the theory.

The photograph was taken by Dave Hogan and is shared with permission.

References

Anderson, H. & Goolishian, H. (1992). The client is the expert: A not-knowing approach to therapy. In McNamee, S. & Gergen, K. J. (Eds.), Inquiries in social construction. Therapy as social construction, pp.25-39. Thousand Oaks, CA, US: Sage Publications, Inc.

Bavelas, J. B. (2012). Connecting the Lab to the Therapy Room. In Franklin C., Trepper, T. S., Gingerich W. J., McCollum E. E. (Eds.), Solution-Focused Brief Therapy, a Handbook of Evidence-Based Practice. Oxford Press.

Bavelas, J. B., Korman, H., DeJong, P., Smock Jordan, S. (2014). Does SFBT Have a Theory? Plenary at the EBTA conference in Leuwaarden.

Bavelas, J. B., Korman, H., DeJong, P., Smock Jordan, S. (2014). The theoretical and research basis of co-constructing meaning in dialogue. Journal of Solution-Focused Brief Therapy. Vol 1, No 2, pp.1-24.

Berg, I. K. & De Jong, P. (1996). Solution-Building Conversations: Co-Constructing a Sense of Competence with Clients. Families in Society: The Journal of Contemporary Human Services. Families International, pp.377-391.

Berg, I. K. & Dolan, Y. (2001). Tales of solutions: A collection of hope-inspiring stories. New York: Norton.

Berger, P. L., Luckmann, T., Zifonum, D. (2002). The social construction of reality. Penguin Books.

Beyebach, M. (2008). "Nothing is better": constructing improvements in solution-focused sessions. Workshop at the EBTA conference in Lyon.

Cecchin, G. (1987). Hypothesising, circularity and neutrality revisited, an invitation to curiosity. Family Process, 26 (4), pp.405–13

Clark, H.H. & Brennan, S. E. (1991). Grounding in communication. In Resnick, L. B., Levine, J. M., Teasley, J. S. D. Perspectives on socially shared cognition. American Psychological Association.

De Jong, P. & Kim Berg, I. (2012). Interviewing for Solutions. Wadsworth Publishing Co Inc.

De Jong P., Bavelas, J. B., Korman, H. (2013). An introduction to using microanalysis to observe co-construction in psychotherapy. Journal of Systemic Therapies, Vol. 32, No.3, 2013, pp.17-30.

de Shazer, S. (1984). The Death of resistance. Family Process, volume 23, Issue 1, pp.11–17.

de Shazer, S. (1991). Putting difference to work. New York: Norton.

de Shazer, S. (1994). Words were originally magic. New York: Norton.

de Shazer, S., Dolan, Y. M., Korman, H., Trepper, T. S., McCollum, E. E., & Berg, I. K. (2006). More than miracles: The state of the art of solution focused therapy. New York: Haworth Press.

EBTA Practice Definition (2012). http://blog.ebta.nu/wp-content/uploads/2012/05/EBTA-SF-PRACTICE-DEFINITIONS_2012.pdf read 31.7.2020.

Erickson, M. H. (1954a). Special techniques of brief hypnotherapy. Journal of clinical and Experimental Hypnosis, 2, pp.109-129.

Erickson, M. H. (1954b). Pseudo-Orientation in time as a hypno therapeutical procedure. Journal of Clinical and Experimental Hypnosis, 2, pp.261-283.

Erickson, M. (1980). The collected papers of Milton H. Erickson: Vol. II. Hypnotic alteration of sensory, perceptual and psychophysiological processes. Irvington.

Fichte, J. G. (1794), Grundlage der gesamten Wissenschaftslehre. Fundamental Principles of the Entire Science of Knowledge. https://voices.uchicago.edu/germanphilosophy/files/2012/05/Fichte-The-Science-of-Knowledge-sec-1-3.pdf read 31.7.2020.

Flatt, S. & Curtis, S. (2013). Offering expert knowledge within a not-knowing solution-focused paradigm: A contradiction in terms or a helpful response to (some) real life conundrums? International Journal of Solution-Focused Practices, Vol 1, No 1, pp.28-30.

Fredrickson, B. (2013). Love 2.0. Penguin Books.

Freud, S; Breuer, J. (1895). Studien über Hysterie. Franz Deuticke, Leipzig & Wien 1895.

Froerer A. & Connie, E. (2016). Solution-Building, The Foundation of Solution-Focused Brief Therapy: A Qualitative Delphi Study. Journal of Family Psychotherapy, vol 27, 2016, Issue 1, pp.20-34.

Gassmann, D. & Grawe, K. (2006). General change mechanisms: The relation between problem activation and resource activation in successful and unsuccessful therapeutic interactions. Clinical Psychology & Psychotherapy 13(1), pp.1 – 11.

George, Evan, (2010). What are the disadvantages of the brief solution focused approach? https://www.brief.org.uk/resources/faq/disadvantages-of-solution-focus read 31.7.2020.

Gingerich, W. J. & Eisengart, S. (2004). Solution focused brief therapy: a review of the outcome research. Family Process 39, pp.477-498.

Hacking, I. (1999). The social construction of what? Harvard University Press.

Haley, J. (1986). Uncommon Therapy. New York: Norton.

Hoyt, M. F. (2001). A conversation with Steve de Shazer and John Weakland. In: Interviews with brief therapy experts, Philadelphia.

Isebaert, L. (2015). Solution-Focused cognitive and systemic therapy: The Bruges Model. London: Routledge.

Iveson, C. & McKergow, M. (2016). Brief Therapy: Focused description development. Journal of Solution-Focused Brief Therapy, Vol 2, No 1, pp.1-17.

Jackson, P. Z. & McKergow, M. (2007). The Solutions Focus, Making coaching & change simple. WS Bookwell.

Kant, I. (1914). Critique of pure reason, translated by Müller, F. M. (2nd ed. revised), London: Macmillan.https://oll.libertyfund.org/titles/ller-critique-of-pure-reason read 31.7.2020.

Korman, H. (2017). The 3.0 version of Reflections on SFBT 2.0. https://www.academia.edu/38423866/The_3.0_version_of_Reflections_on_SFBT_2.0.pdf read 31.7.2020.

Korzybski, A. (1933). Science and Sanity. Institute for General Semantics.

Kramer, U. & Stiles, W. B. (2015). The responsiveness problem in psychotherapy: A review of proposed solutions. Clinical Psychology: Science and Practice, 22, pp.277-295.

Lauth, R. (1989). Die transzendentale Konstitution der gesellschaftlichen Erfahrung. In: Transzendentale Entwicklungslinien von Descartes bis zu Marx und Dostojewski, Hamburg: Meiner.

Levinson, S. C. (2017). Speech Acts. In Huang, Y. (Ed.), The Oxford Handbook of Pragmatics.

Hutto, D.D. & Myin, E. (2012): Radicalizing enactivism. The MIT Press.

Lipton, P. (2001). Inference to the Best Explanation, London: Routledge

Lütterfelds, W. (1989). Fichte und Wittgenstein: Der thetische Satz, Stuttgart: Klett-Cotta.

Macdonald, A. (2017). Solution-focused Brief Therapy evaluation list, http://blog.ebta.nu/wp-content/uploads/2017/12/SFTOCT2017.pdf read 31.7.2020.

Mattila, A. (2001). Seeing things in a new light. Reframing in therapeutic conversation. University of Helsinki, Faculty of Medicine, Institute of Clinical Medicine.

McGee, Del Vento, & Bavelas, J.B. (2005). An interactional model of questions as therapeutic interventions. Journal of Marital and Family Therapy, October 2005, Vol 31, No 4, pp.371-384.

McKergow, M. & Korman, H. (2009). In between - neither inside nor outside: The radical simplicity of Solution-Focused Brief Therapy. Journal of Systemic Therapies, pp.34–49.

McKergow, M. (2016). Solution-Focused practice: Engaging with the client as a first-person, rather than a third person. InterAction, Volume 8, number 1: pp.31-44.

McKergow, M. (2016.) SFBT 2.0: The next generation of Solution Focused Brief Therapy has already arrived, Journal of Solution Focused Brief Therapy vol 2 no 2, pp.1-17.

McKergow, M. (2020). Stretching the World. In Dierolf, K., Hogan, D., van der Hoorn,S., Wignaraja (Eds), Solution Focused Practice Around the World. Routledge, 2020

McLeod, J., McLeod, J., Shoemark, Al., Cooper, M. (2009). User constructed outcomes: Therapeutic practice and everyday life. Paper presented at the Psychotherapeutic Practice Research Conference, University of Jyväskylä, February 2009.

Miller, G. & de Shazer, S. (1998). Have You Heard the Latest Rumor About ...? Solution-Focused Therapy as a Rumor. Family Process 37, pp.363-378

Miller, G. (2008). Loughborough Group (Discursive Psychology) and Ethnomethodology, Karlstad Group, 2nd Meeting, Vienna: March 25-26, 2008.

Miller, G. & McKergow, M. (2012). From Wittgenstein, Complexity, and Narrative Emergence: Discourse and Solution-Focused Brief Therapy . In Lock, A. & T. Strong, T. (Eds.) Discursive Perspectives in Therapeutic Practice. Oxford: Oxford University Press), pp.163-183.

Miller, G. (2014). Culture in Solution-Focused consultation: An intercultural approach. Journal of Solution-Focused Brief Therapy. Vol 1, No 2, pp.25-40.

Minuchin, S. (1974). Families and family therapy. Cambridge: Harvard University Press.

Morris, D. R. (2005). Causal inference in the social sciences: Variance theory, process theory, and system dynamics. https://proceedings.systemdynamics.org/2005/proceed/papers/MORRI261.pdf read 31.7.2020.

Nylund, D. & Corsiglia, V. (1994). Becoming Solution-Focused Forced in Brief Therapy: Remembering Something Important We Already Knew. Journal of Systemic Therapies: Vol. 13, No. 1, pp.5-12.

Nunnally, E., de Shazer, S., Lipchik, E., Berg, I. K. (1986). A Study of change: Therapeutic theory in process. In Efron D. E. (Ed.) Journeys: Expansion of the Strategic-Systemic Therapies, New York: Brunner/Mazel.

Raz , J. (2017). Intention and value, Philosophical Explorations, 20:sup2, pp.109-126.

Ryan, R. M. & Deci, E. L. (2000). Self-determination theory and the facilitation of intrinsic motivation, social development, and wellbeing. American Psychologist, 55, pp.68-78.

Panayotow, P. (2020). Solution is Only a Smile Away. https://www.academia.edu/30941198/Solution_Is_Only_a_Smile_Away read 31.7.2020.

Prada, A. S. & Beyebach, M. (2008). "Nothing is better": Constructing improvements in solution-focused sessions. Presentation at the EBTA conference 2008.

Peräkylä, A., Antaki, C., Vehviläinen, S., Leudar, I., (2008). Conversation analysis and psychotherapy. Cambridge University Press.

Rappaport, J., Swift, C. F., Hess, R. (1984). Studies in empowerment: Steps toward understanding and action. New York: Haworth Press.

Rogers, C. (1951). Client-Centered Therapy. Cambridge Massachusetts: The Riverside Press.

Seligman, M. (2011). Flourish, A new understanding of happiness and well-being and how to achieve them. Nicholas Brealy.

Selvini-Palazzoli, M., Boscol, L., Cecchin G., Prata, G., (1973). Paradox and Counterparadox. New York: Aronson.

Shennan, G., (2016). Extended mind, extended person, extended therapy? InterAction vol.8 nr 1 2016, pp.7-30..

Shennan, G. (2017). Comments on the draft for theory of solution-focused practice. September 2017.

Shick, R. (2017). Solution-Focused Brief Therapy from the client's perspective: A Descriptive phenomenological analysis. Athabasca University.

Solution Focused Therapy Treatment Manual for Working with Individuals, 2nd version, (2013). Research Committee of the Solution Focused Brief Therapy Association. https://irp-cdn.multis-creensite.com/f39d2222/files/uploaded/Treatment%20Manual%20-Final%2C%20Update%203-17-18.pdf read 31.07.2020.

The Solution-Focused Collective, (2019). A Solution-Focused Manifesto for Social Change. https://solfocollective.net/the-manifesto-for-text-readers/ read 31.7.2020.

Thomas, F., (2016). Complimenting in Solution-Focused Brief Therapy. Journal of Solution-Focused Brief Therapy, Vol 2, No1.

UKASFP Accreditable Practice and Accreditable Practitioners, 2015.

von Foerster, H. & Pörksen, B. (2002). Understanding systems, conversations on epistemology and ethics. Heidelberg: Carl-Auer-Systeme Verlag.

Walter, J. L. & Peller, J. E. (1992). Becoming Solution-Focused in Brief Therapy. Routledge.

Watzlawick, P. (Ed.) (1980). The Invented Reality: How Do We Know What We Believe We Know?. New York: Norton.

Watzlawick, P. (1988). Ultra Solutions. How to fail most successfully. New York: Norton.

Wells, J. (2018). Ni inspirerar mig. Lösningsfokuserade förantaganden till stöd för bättre samtal och möten. Södra Dalarnas Samordningsförbund. Exakta. Malmö.

Weakland, J. H., Watzlawick, P., Fisch, R., (1974). Change: Principles of problem formation and problem resolution. New York: WW Norton.

Weakland, J. H., Fisch, R., Watzlawick, P., Bodin, A. M. (1974). Brief Therapy: Focused Problem Resolution. Family Process, 13, pp.141–168.

Wittgenstein, L. (1922). Tractatus logico-philosophicus. Routledge.

Wittgenstein, L. (1953). Philosophical investigations. Basil Blackwell.

Wittgenstein, L. (1969). On certainty. Basil Blackwell.

Personal
Reflections ...

Reflective Reviews on the

Theory of Solution-Focused Practice

2020 Version, by

Thorana Nelson

Alasdair J. Macdonald

Arild Aambø

Sukanya Wignaraja

Guy Shennan

Tomasz Switek

Thorana Nelson

I. Overview

Your group process has done a great job of describing SF practice in both context (stance, assumptions, etc.) and practice. It is well organized, well written, and reasonably easy to understand. I'm not sure about the audience. If it's SF practitioners, I think it organizes our thinking well. If it's for non-SF folks, it includes some confusing or not-well-defined ideas, which I will comment on later. It seems from the introduction that your aim is for both groups, perhaps more for the former or those who are intrigued and want to understand the overall philosophy better.

II. Theory

Although you have labeled this as theory, my earlier training in family science and philosophy of science leads me to some confusion. What is written is very clear about process theory, describing the approach without going into detail on the oft-repeated concepts and practices. For those who are inclined to quibble about theory and Theory, it might be useful to contrast process theory (descriptive; how something develops) with the notion of theory that explains something and includes hypotheses and/or testable constructs. I think it's the latter that Steve opposed so much. The former is more descriptive and based on observations than explaining why something is the way it is (e.g., one of my theories about SFBP is that scaling helps people organize their thinking and picture a better life, thus reducing anxiety, which allows their thinking processes to work toward their goals – a la Bowen; others have different ideas about how SFBP works, Steve didn't even want to think about it beyond language/ Wittgenstein).

You state that "in the SF world, theory is only as useful as it is pragmatic. It should enable research, support practitioners, and enhance the quality of service to clients." One thing that process omits is notions of interlinking constructs and testable hypotheses (reasons something works the way it seems to). This addresses what you are not attempting in this paper.

This basically is descriptive theory with some underpinning philosophy rather than explanatory theory. Am I getting your idea?

I like the idea of abduction – I have never heard of that. As describing the oscillation between observable practice patterns and abstract ideas, I think you have hit the nail on the head. This is where I think a number of people have become confused, especially if they were trained in "theories" (which more rightly should be called approaches) and want to know more about the theory of SFBP. Placing your ideas in this context, which I think could be highlighted more in some way, really helps both those wanting to know more about the practice or approach and those who want to or even insist on knowing more about the philosophy, explanation of how/why it works, etc. This also makes me think about dialectics, where there are seemingly two contradictory ideas (in this case, explanation vs description) that one struggles with, culminating in a synthesis that includes neither and both. I think you have done that successfully.

Your diagram of practice within a cube of theory and description is interesting, as is the notion that as practice expands, so must theory and description. I understand about description (e.g., the use of "best hopes" as it emerged beyond the miracle question) and think the theory-expansion part is very important, but only if it fits within a larger structure of philosophy that opposes negation of any of the basic assumptions of the SF stance. To go further would require a different structure, philosophy, way of thinking. So, do some of our colleagues' ideas that are expansions still fit within the overall "family" of SF?

III. Being in context

As someone who was trained in system thinking (von Bertalanffy) and cybernetics, I am delighted to see how you have woven these important relational ideas into this work without raising unnecessary flags for those who think of "systems" as a particular practice. Relational contexts are incredibly important and too often ignored by people who use the practices of SFBP (Solution Focused Brief Practices) without understanding much of what you are writing about. Context was one of the important foci of change that Steve described, practiced, and wrote about. Including many aspects of clients' contexts, especially personal relationships, I believe, is necessary to the stance but seldom discussed. This leaves many to see SFB practices in linear ways rather than understanding the nuance of clients' troubles and solutions systemically, as embedded in context.

One aspect of context that is not described, however, is the client-therapist relationship. We try to keep ourselves out of the picture, but as second-order cybernetics would suggest, we are part of the clients' systems and need to acknowledge that, not in the least so that we don't overly influence directions the client may go. Using our own ideas judiciously and tentatively helps, but I think that placing it clearly within the clients' context may help us stay on the periphery. I like it when clients can't remember my name but would hope that they can remember something of what we did together, especially in terms of meaning, either in thinking or doing.

Which leads to ideas about change. Steve and Insoo were clearly steeped in notions of change as centering on thinking and/or doing and their recursive nature. They also realized that the work emphasizes the recursive nature of change between thinking and doing, and also that change is recursively situated with other elements of the clients' context such as noticing and emphasizing how context supports (or doesn't support) change. This may mean other people, internalized values and customs, and systemic biases and actions. This latter aspect – contextual response to change – is often missed in my experience. A client may consider that the changes they seek are at an 8 and therefore sufficient for the moment. Also, the client may be aware of contextual factors that limit further "progress" in the totality of their life, things that practitioners may not understand. If someone or something in the client's context is non-supportive – either actively or inactively, changes the client deemed sufficient may suddenly turn sour. This is another reason to actively include context, whether others participate in the interview or not. Systemically, these potential "gotchas" or "yes, buts" are more easily anticipated and used in the service of desired change when those others participate in therapy or at least when the client and practitioner discuss them and the potential consequences of change. Thus, the importance of relational questions: Who would notice? What would they see? What difference would that make to them? What difference would that make to you? It is too easy for us to presume that the observed differences would be acceptable to the other person and the client. Rather, we might inquire about other changes that would be more acceptable to the client.

IV. Explanation and meaning

„Changing meaning" – you refer to the SF stance, but this is the first time. Should it be expanded somewhat somewhere?

"Making sense of perceptions" – This is a tough one, something that requires we keep our own ideas out of the way. Sometimes, this means voicing them either to clients or colleagues, but doing something to get them out of our own heads (except as it might be useful, e.g., if we genuinely think of something the client does not know or is not aware of).

You have made your thoughts about pertinent Wittgenstein ideas and how they inform our work in a very clear and helpful way.

In general, your thoughts about meaning are great. The notion of co-construction of meaning is not very clear, though. I'm not sure where that could go, but I think it's confusing to those who are not familiar with post-structuralism and philosophy in general. I think this is very important, expanding people's understanding of meaning as not intractable and as created in context, not solely in their heads. This applies to relationships with important others in terms of how their meanings may negate clients' ideas, or, at the least, be confusing to the client. Further, in terms of supporting desired change, new meanings in the clients' lives must include some sort of co-construction with others, not just the practitioner. Similarly, under changing direction, you note the client-centric aspects of change, taking their values, etc. as "the base for the help," could include a context-centric emphasis as well – the values, worldviews, and experiences of the client's social context, including larger systems such as education, politics, and health care.

I have a bit of a problem with the idea that everyone is capable of living a meaningful life, at least as stated here. I do believe that all human beings have worth and capacity, but sometimes, their contexts don't allow for much. I'm thinking of refugees particularly.

Building with confidence and resilience – well done! In my experience, too many practitioners believe they stand above their clients in some way and, without meaning to, negate clients' capacities and resources, or think there are better ones.

I also very much appreciate the notions given about attending to consequences of changes. One of the criticisms I have heard about SFBP is that we somehow do not consider untoward consequences, leaving it to the client to bang into something without warning when we have our own and others' experiences to suggest (tentatively, of course). I have had a number of clients who changed goals somewhat after thinking through the potential negative consequences of their changes. Others have determined that settling for less than 10 is ok because of the balance of different aspects of their lives, how those are affected by change, and how they may respond.

V. Main assumptions, values, and beliefs

I don't recall anything in de Shazer et al., 2007, about mediation as offered to help clients in conflict. That doesn't mean it's not there, I just don't recall it.

I disagree that SF doesn't have a theory of the development of client abilities. I think it does through the expansion of clients' beliefs, actions, meanings – expanded opportunities and or understanding, expansion of the thinking and doing readily available to clients. Also, our strong belief in our clients' capacities to know what changes are best for them, to act on them, and to co-construct meaning from them. Of course, these are more clearly explicated in other theories such as social psychology, etc., but I think are implicit in our stance about people and change.

I like the map metaphor. Maps, of necessity, omit much information. Our professional stance of curiosity helps us elucidate omissions that may be helpful but not noticed by clients.

I suggest care when writing about "positivity." It is taken in so many ways, especially by so-called positive psychology, that many practitioners believe they are solution-focused because the focus on positives or strengths. I think your work clearly points out that this is not the center of our work. If all we do is point out positives, we risk missing a lot of resources as well as leaving the client feeling not heard. Nothing else in that section points toward positivity per se, so I think it's best to either elucidate or omit.

Connecting with the client's language is so important, even when formulating additions in turn-taking. Language, itself, is a very big word, encompassing more than words, but the way they are put together, the values and beliefs they suggest, reflexivity of context, possibilities and impossibilities, etc. I think an example of "using the client's core concepts and logic" might clarify things a bit. Otherwise, my experience in trainings and supervision is that learners think this means only words and only literal meanings of words (or the subjective meanings they ascribe to clients' words, which often leads to all sorts of inaccuracies or oversights).

I love that you point out that there often is much in "small intricate details" in clients' descriptions. Nuance, opportunities for alternate meanings, etc. come forth through our curiosity and questions, requests for details even when clients think they are "banal."

Offering suitable support – this is where I believe taking context and important others into account is very important. The notion of support can be co-constructed between practitioner and client, but I believe works better when co-constructed between the client and important others affected by change.

Hurrah for mentioning that client competence may be hidden or lying dormant! As practitioners, we must be faithful to our beliefs in client competence and actively search for it when clients are particularly discouraged, confused, or flummoxed.

Noticing and amplifying progress: this is a place where you could emphasize the need to identify client agency in change. How did they make something happen, or how did they support something, or what can they do to keep it going? An example would be helpful.

I hope these comments add a few ideas that may be helpful and I am so grateful of all the people who have put so much energy and thought into this paper.

Alasdair J. Macdonald

This document seems to me to be a valuable contribution to the literature about solution-focused practice. It represents work by world leaders within this discipline over the best part of ten years. The current study group supported by the *European Brief Therapy Association* (EBTA) includes nine well-known practitioners, representing eight countries. Two of these practitioners were founder members of EBTA. In previous years other leading workers have been members of this group. The authors also quote the opinions of many other well-known authorities.

The project has been given much time by EBTA members at most of their international meetings.They have drawn on the skills of the existing group members as well as the ideas presented by other workers at the international conferences and other major meetings. The resulting document presented here is a clear and helpful account of the central ideas currently included in solution-focused practice around the world. As will be seen, many of these ideas area also outlined in similar documents from other countries such as the guidance given by the *Solution-Focused Brief Therapy Association* of North America.

There is long-standing debate about solution-focused therapy as a practice, with or without a theory of change. Many publications exist which have attempted to relate this form of practice to the effectiveness or otherwise of other forms of therapy. Also, many publications exist which try to relate solution-focused practice to the many references made within the philosophical ideas presented in the work of Wittgenstein. Wittgenstein's work is a landmark in the use of language in human communication and in language as a way of constructing meaning in our cognitive understanding of the human world.

Steve de Shazer was widely regarded by many academic philosophers as an exceptional thinker in relation to Wittgenstein's ideas. However, the existence of so many views in the attempt to describe solution-focused therapy may imply that we are missing the point somewhere. Perhaps we are not yet equal to the level of discourse required to represent solution-focused practice clearly.

Solution-focused ideas and techniques are widely used in management and organisational work. They have proved remarkably successful in these settings. There is a substantial body of literature reporting projects and research studies concerning solution-focused applications in the workplace. Unlike the therapy world, there seems to be little rivalry between these applications and the many other organisational tools available to the commercial world. A successful practitioner will find employment and profit whether they use solution-focused ideas or some other model of working. Talking about "payment by results" seems a rather facile way to summarize this difference but it is a well-established business mantra.

The *EBTA Evaluation List* of research studies extends from 1995 until 03/11/17. Google Scholar finds more than 2800 publications annually in English and at least 12 other languages. The valid existing material in 2017 included 10 meta-analyses; 7 systematic reviews; 325 relevant outcome studies including 143 randomised controlled trials showing benefit from solution-focused approaches with 92 showing benefit over existing treatments. Of 100 comparison studies, 71 favoured SFT. Effectiveness data were also available from over 9000 cases with a success rate exceeding 60%; requiring an average of 3 to 6.5 sessions of therapy time.

In the United States of America the model is approved by the US Federal Government: SAMHSA-The National Registry of Evidence-based Programs and Practices (NREPP).[1] As regards other states, the State of Washington and the State of Oregon have approved it.[2] The State of Texas is examining evidence. Minnesota, Michigan and California have organisations using solution-focused brief approaches. Finland has an MSc in Solution-Focused Therapy (awarded in England) and Singapore has an approved accreditation programme. Canada has a registration body for practitioners and therapists. South Korea has a certificated training course and a journal in the relevant language. Sweden, Poland, Germany and Austria recognize it within their systemic practice qualifica-

---

[1] Retrieved from https://www.nrepp.samhsa.gov/landing.asp; 2018, May 18.

[2] www.oregon.gov/DHS

tion. Wales (UK) includes it in their primary mental health programme.

Arild Aambø

I have enjoyed reading the latest version of the *Theory of Solution Focused Practice*. It is indeed an impressive work, a comprehensive collection of views neatly put together to a challenging document. Especially, I liked the paragraph on *The main assumptions, values and beliefs* at page 42, as it to a great extent corresponds with my own views. Still, it makes me think: *"What are the uses of The main assumptions, values and beliefs?"* Do such statements work as premises for logically derived arguments?

This prompts the next question: *"Is SF-practice built on such theoretical constructions?"* Obviously not. To my understanding, Steve built his model from studying videos of Insoo´s and others spontaneous, creative work, focusing on what differences make a difference, only later linking it to a philosophy of language. Could it be that *The main assumptions, values and beliefs* serve as guidelines, supporting and inspiring our clinical work? Here, my answer seems to be: "Perhaps, at least for some." Should they be presented to the clients as a different view of the world in order to facilitate change? Or, do such statements serve just as anchors or connections to some larger or deeper discussions which we leave untouched? Is it a way to explain our practice to other people, or is it something that we just have to accept and accommodate to in order to become real SF-therapists? Such questions inspire me to offer some alternative views, largely influenced by my experiences working as physician, facilitator and researcher regarding health issues among the great diversity of immigrants to Norway during the latest decades, and, not least, by my concern regarding some extreme cases of violence that have taken place both among natives and immigrants.

First, an assumption that I feel is very important is that *change is inevitable*. This is also alluded to in page 44. It is therefore a bit surprising for me to find that nearly every time change is mentioned in the document, which is quite often, it is presented *as if* clients are stuck with no change and *as if* status quo is the rule, and therapist as well as client must take effort in order to create change.

Second, today, there is considerable support for a *biology of cognition* that assumes that all life is purposive in the sense that creatures at all levels direct their actions towards goals; goals such as fulfilling a need, or, at a meta level, restraining oneself from such strivings. Most humans have the capacity to choose between goals, and this choice installs a sense of responsibility, a responsibility for preserving life's purposiveness, which seems to be unique to humans. The sense of responsibility adds to our worth as human beings, and, according to Hans Jonas, when we act in ways that make it more difficult for others to take on their responsibility, we act unethically.

If Jonas, Maturana and many others who have discussed these issues are right, to be goal directed (and thus also solution oriented) actually is the natural stance for human beings. However, sometimes, when the purposiveness is combined with executive power and implementation force derived of any sense of other people's needs and responsibility, what I tend to call unmitigated agency, great harm can be done to nature as well as to the social surroundings. Thus, our problem as human beings is usually not that we are lacking goals and purpose. The challenge is to choose between goals in order to pursue those that are most satisfying, gratifying and ethically acceptable.

As therapists, our concern should be that some people might have fallen victims for changes that they have not asked for, changes that typically do not fit, and which leave them with a sense of confusion and powerlessness, thus momentarily hampering or paralysing their purposiveness. Among other things, this can be a result of other peoples unmitigated agency. I assume that in many such cases, an empowering process facilitated and stimulated by solution-focused questions is highly appropriate. Here, I understand empowerment not as emancipation, but as a process to stimulate motivation to relate to or even cope with unwanted changes.

Empowerment might restore purposiveness, help people to gain trust and confidence in their own competency and motivate people to take more control in their lives. Working with immigrant women from Pakistan and some other highly patriarchal societies, however, I often experienced that this was not a straightforward process. Patriarchy is oppressive, but it also offers great possibilities for protection, which many of these women depend on and which they are willing to pay for by sacrificing influence over certain domains.

The empowering process mentioned several times and well described in the 2020 version of the SF-theory, where also a lot is said about stimulating the clients agency. Visualising a better future is obviously important for all of us. However, so is visualising potentially harmful consequences of our actions, especially those unintended and which we are unaware of. We all know how unmitigated agency and solipsistic strivings can be harmful and lead us astray, and therefore, we need to question whether stimulating a persons agency is appropriate in all situations and in all the different domains in which SF-practice is introduced. What I find missing is a clearer emphasis on other peoples perspectives, whether these people are significant others or unknown to us, but potential victims of our agency. Put differently, I feel that it is not completely sound to introduce empowerment without a more thorough discussion on power issues.

A more balanced view can be obtained by asking relationship questions, which when properly used are equally well suited to clarify social support and mitigate agency. It is also important that therapists help their clients to reflect on values and attitudes. Although not completely neglected, I think such questions and considerations have got far too little emphasis in the document. As I remember it, when Insoo still was in her family practice, she told that she used an SF-approach in about 80% of her cases. In the end, it is a question about the limitations of SF-practice, on which I find no mention in the theory draft. After more than 40 years of practice, this is still an unanswered question, although it might have highly ethical implications.

I agree that the terms *customer*, *complainer* and *visitor* now is left out, as the connotations are not well suited to support an SF-practice. However, I miss a discussion on the relationship between client and therapist – how this relationship can be understood, and the necessity of creating trust in order for words and utterings to be taken in their best sense.

Finally, although misunderstandings might be the rule and, if revealed, can be quite stimulating and offer creative opportunities, I think it is wise to work towards a shared understanding of the situation as well as of the problem and the solution. Is shared understanding an issue in SF-work?

Moreover, what happened to the scaling questions? Numbers, with all their pitfalls, can still be an excellent and very precise expression that facilitates a shared understanding.

References

Aambø, A. (2014). "One Heart, Many Hands" Reflections on diversity, relationships, and expanding conversations. Fokus på Familien, 1-2014, pp.49–71.

Jonas, H. (1981). The Imperative of Responsibility – In Search of an Ethics for the Technological Age. Chicago: The University of Chicago Press.

Maturana, H. R. & Varela, F. J. (1987). The Tree of Knowledge – The Biological Roots of Human Understanding Boston: Shambala Publications.

Sukanya Wignaraja

My introduction to solution focused practice came a little over a decade ago. It was an eye-opener, a very different way of "doing" therapy and challenged much of what I knew back then. I was, like many newbies, sceptical but at the same time curious. I was fortunate also to have an excellent teacher and mentor in Debbie Hogan who guided me and patiently answered my questions. Debbie told us the story of how SF developed and I recall being struck by how it was born out of practice, how the theory of it came later and I had the sense that theory was somehow less crucial in the understanding of how solution focused practice worked. Subsequent discussions with peers over the years left me feeling the need for a clearly-articulated theory, not only for those of us within the SF community but also something that we could point people towards, whether critics or those curious to know more. This document has filled that gap and I am grateful to the EBTA task group for producing this.

As with any model, SF has its critics but there is now a growing body of research that demonstrates its efficacy and outcomes. A theory acts not only as a reference point for practitioners but also as clear explanation of what we do, how and why. When I first began using SF in my therapy practice, I would keep a list of questions (many of us did this), which functioned like a cross between a script and an aide memoire. Today, that script is no longer necessary as the questions have become second nature. As I read through this document, it made me think again about how I work, the rationale behind what I do and also the way in which SF has become firmly embedded in the way I approach many things, not only my work. SF, as we all know, appears deceptively simple but it requires a disciplined mindset and an understanding of the rationale to maintain that simplicity. This document sets out that rationale in a clear and accessible way. I specially appreciated the section on "Changing meaning" which explains complex philosophical ideas in the context of SF practice.

The assumptions and beliefs of SF lie at the heart of what we do and that particular section of the document is, in my view, one of the most important. It also highlights another aspect of SF practice, the language we use: the seemingly simple questions which are actually carefully constructed, and intentional. Clients sometimes pick up on this and comment that the questions are "different", "interesting" or they will say "nobody has ever asked me that before". It is very helpful to have a succinct summary of how these assumptions and beliefs link in with the way practitioners then make sense of the client's world view, their hopes and their belief in their own ability to change, while paying particular attention to the desired future (and this last is unique to SF). This document also highlights another aspect of SF which is often picked upon by critics, that SF is somehow superficial and fails to go "deeper" and neglects the clients´ past. The detailed explanations of how an SF-"conversation" works and the intricate layers therein, go a long way in addressing and refuting such criticisms.

The section on "key topics" is very well put together and once again, it unpacks how SF practitioners work with clients and illustrates the richness of the model. And of course, one of the unique features of SF is that it is used with equal success in a therapeutic context as well as with teams, organisations and in corporate settings. This aspect is highlighted throughout.

This document is an excellent resource in the way it brings together the theory and practice of SF and it is an important addition to the SF canon. While it will be welcomed by practitioners and trainers, a wider circulation outside the SF community is also essential.

Guy Shennan

I am honoured to have been invited by the EBTA Practice Definition Group to write some reflections on the *Theory of Solution-Focused Practice*. First, I want to congratulate the group on their longevity and persistence, as I read that their work began in 2007. Although this might make it appear that their work has not been brief, this of course does not follow. I am sure they have not had one meeting more than has been necessary! I note that other documents have been produced along the way, for example the *EBTA Practice Definition* in 2012. I have to say that I do not recall this, though I am sure it will have been the subject of discussion at EBTA conferences and meetings. I mention this now to contrast my impression of this document, which through the efforts of the group, both at and in between conferences, has developed a noticeable profile. I congratulate the group on this too, on how they have brought their work to our attention, and encouraged our engagement with it. It is a living, breathing document, whose collective provenance is clear. I am referring here not only to the nine authors named on the front, but also to the way those authors have involved a wider solution-focused community in the work's development. There is a fitting photograph of many more of the document's contributors at the end of the document, under the appropriate heading: "Expanding the circle of ideas". The footnotes, too, a number of which refer to comments made on earlier drafts, and the changes made to the document itself, attest to the collective efforts that have created it. Finally, I congratulate the group on the document itself.

Its collective development fits with the culture which originally produced solution-focused brief therapy in Milwaukee in the early 1980s. In recent years, together with one of the task group members, Kirsten Dierolf, I have had a number of conversations with some of the people who were at the Brief Family Therapy Center in the early days, and the importance of teamwork to the development of the solution-focused approach has been clear. In their conclusion, the task group refer to the "culture of curiosity" at Milwaukee, and to the "sharing and debate which helped to bring the approach into being". I believe that the group's hope that their work will continue to nourish such a culture, "to keep the approach alive and open to change", is being realized, and that this will contribute to the "further spirals of evolution" they also hope for.

It is perhaps unsurprising that the collective nature of this work has presented itself forcefully to me, given my own current interests. In an earlier attempt at theory development, when Steve de Shazer (1994) was trying to make sense of Milton Erickson's work, he considered the effects of his decision to interpret Erickson's case examples as stories. He explained how his role as "reader" then entered the process, and "the unit of investigation switched from (1) Erickson and his papers to (2) Erickson, his papers, and me" (de Shazer, 1994, p32). Similarly, as I reflect on the task group's *Theory of Solution-Focused Practice*, what I am actually doing is reflecting on this theory, and me. This can be seen as an example of the "interactional view" (Watzlawick & Weakland, 1977), which permeates the task group's theory (an aspect of which, a little paradoxically perhaps, I shall later gently challenge).

So, reflecting on this theory (or Theory) through the prism of my own interests, and as a member of the *Solution-Focused Collective* (2019), it was good to see the Collective being mentioned, albeit in a footnote, and references made to environmental and political factors. Though these are only thinly described, and mainly feature as part of an individual client's background, they are welcome pointers to some potential "spirals of evolution". For example, it is assumed that "change happens in the client's social context... (t)herefore many questions are about preferred changes in the relationships and the environment at hand" (p13). The footnote mentioning the Collective is attached to a reference to the client's "power to influence", and refers to the ambiguity associated with "empowerment" (p11). This ambiguity is present here, with empowerment being seen as an invitation to the client to become aware of their power, or agency, and is "mostly personal empowerment", though also includes interpersonal and socio-political empowerment (p10). The last of these is said to be about accessing resources and "questioning commonly held truths", which sounds interesting though would benefit from some further elucidation and illustration.

There is a hint of an advocate's role in "accessing resources", while the questioning part reminded me of the way that a narrative therapist might deconstruct a "dominant discourse" impacting on a client's life. I might be going further here than the authors intended, but I think there is further to go.

In an interesting related passage in the introductory section, the effects on a client of their membership of many groups are discussed, and also the effects on those groups of changes in the client. It is suggested that "client" could refer to a group or organisation as well as an individual, but more clarity would help. The passage ends with the comment "SF practice honours the individual within the interactional web", which I think it very much does, but then curiously adds "without privileging the individual over the collective" (p17). I think the individual *is* privileged in the theory, which as presented here is of a largely individualistic endeavour, notwithstanding the references in Part 1 to the wider, non-therapeutic contexts in which the solution-focused approach is now used. The world could do with changing, as well as individuals within it, and surely a solution-focused approach could help with this too. As the footnote on the *Solution-Focused Collective* implies, we should avoid translating public issues into private troubles, and as solution-focused practitioners we need to be on our guard against colluding with such translations as much as any other purportedly helping professionals.

Having referred to the world or individuals within it changing, let me offer some reflections on this idea of change. I sometimes begin workshops by inviting participants to call out one word that they think might be most central to the solution-focused approach. It is an activity not to be taken too seriously, as I do not think there is any particular word at the centre of the approach, but it is a nice way to create energy and get people thinking, and eventually someone will shout out the word "change". If the approach did have a central word, this would be a favourite choice of many. It also leads to the nicely paradoxical SFBT origin story of how someone behind the screen in Milwaukee suggested what was to become the Formula First Session Task - let's ask the client to think about what they DON'T want to change! Then in the next session, the clients reported positive changes in concrete detail. So maybe change is the word, after all. It certainly appears as fundamental in this document, in which it appears 154 times, with solution-focused practice being "an activity of helping clients to change" (p24), and solution-focused conversations focusing on the client's "desired change" (p40-41).

This, however, is not how I think about solution-focused practice. The idea of change suggests changing from one state to another, and so keeps two states in view, which could be thought of as a "problem" and "solution" state respectively. This fits with how the approach was developed, and why it has this name "solution-focused", which now seems an unfortunate one. It is not so much that "solutions" became so overused a word in marketing that the English satirical magazine, *Private Eye*, had a regular column making fun of this (for example, cardboard boxes being sold as "Christmas Ornament Storage Solutions"). It is more that the word does not fit the activity as I understand it and think it has developed, especially from the 1990s onwards. The idea of "solution" suggests that a "problem" is being "solved", just as the idea of change suggests a change from one state to another.

I don't recall ever having this notion in my head, of helping a client change from one state to another - by looking, in part, for exceptions to the first, problem state - since first being trained in SFBT in 1995. I was taught by BRIEF, and, in my view, their streamlining of the approach was already far advanced by then, and they were close to being "beyond solutions", to use the title of their presentation to the 2003 EBTA conference. Looking back now, I believe they were crystallising developments that had already begun at Milwaukee, which Steve de Shazer summarized in an interview with Dan Short (de Shazer and Berg, 1997), by saying that SFBT was "just the miracle question and scaling...". Another part of this jigsaw - in which the pieces were being reduced to a minimum - was a focus on times the miracle picture was already happening supplanting the focus on exceptions (to problems that were no longer being asked about). According to Michele Weiner-Davis, Eve Lipchik was the first in the Milwaukee team to ask about such times (Malinen, 2002), now often known as "instances"[1].

Two more essential jigsaw pieces were Chris Iveson's coining of the question, "What are your best hopes from our work together?", and the miracle picture becoming that of those hopes being realised rather than of the client's problems having gone. The second of these removed the last lingering reference to "problem" from the process, thus enabling the final move beyond solution, while the first suggests what we might find there. My description of the solution-focused process, and perhaps my rationale for it too, would be of a process with *hope* at its centre - or at its beginning might be more accurate - rather than *change*. Rather than, as in this theory, "best hopes" being just one of several ways to describe the client's "best possible change", I see solution-focused practice as enabling an unfolding and shifting articulation of movement, both potential and actual, towards the client's best hopes from the work.

Words matter, and I took a little while over my choice of "enabling" in the sentence above. Some people - including the EBTA Practice Definition Group - might have gone for "co-constructing" instead, following in the large solution-focused footsteps of Insoo Kim Berg, who co-wrote the paper that the group cite as an early forerunner of their attempt to provide a rationale for solution-focused practice (Berg & De Jong,

---

[1] Contrary to the the footnote on page 19, this term was not "coined" by BRIEF. See my blog post for the full story! (Shennan, 2020).

1996). This paper situates SFBT as one of several social constructionist approaches, and it was interesting to re-read it in this context, and to consider the motivations that might have lain behind writing it - and by extension those behind this document. SFBT surely does share features with approaches seen as social constructionist, and it would also be unsurprising if being afforded the intellectual and professional credibility of being seen to share this metatheory were welcome.

I am not convinced that solution-focused practice needs to be situated under a metatheory in this way. Further discussion about this would be helpful, and it clearly connects with the Theory presented here, but I will end with a thought about one specific aspect of social constructionism it uses, the notion of *co-constructing*. I wonder if the social constructionist's keenness to emphasise the importance of the interaction has led to a terminology that over-emphasises the practitioner's role in the generation of what belongs to the client. To facilitate, to enable, to assist, are activities that place us as solution-focused practitioners at the service of our clients, and of their constructions of preferred futures and descriptions of movement towards them.

Similarly, these reflections of mine have been influenced by many people and many readings, prior to reading the Theory document itself, though even if they had been produced via an interview with me, rather than by a solitary tapping at my laptop, they would still have been my thoughts and my responsibility. I hope they might be useful to someone reading them, and thereby have even a little bit of influence in their turn.

References

de Shazer, S. (1994). Words Were Originally Magic. New York: Norton.

de Shazer, S. & Berg, I. K. (1997). An interview by Dan Short with Steve de Shazer and Insoo Kim Berg, Milton H Erickson Foundation Newsletter, 17, 2.

Shennan, G. (2020). What's in a word? Exceptions, instances, assets and unique outcomes. Guy's blog. https://www.guyshennan.com/post/what-s-in-a-word-exceptions-instances-assets-and-unique-outcomes Accessed 12 June 2020

Solution-Focused Collective (2019). The Manifesto. https://solfocollective.net/the-manifesto-for-text-readers/ Accessed 12 June 2020.

Watzlawick, P. & Weakland, J. (1977). The Interactional View. Studies at the Mental Research Institute, 1965-1977. New York: Norton.

Tomasz Switek

In this short review I'll do my best to share with some spontaneous reactions which grown in my mind in reaction to the rich set of ideas presented in "2020 version" of the *Theory of Solution-Focused Practice* presented by the EBTA-Practice Definition Group. Following habits created by Insoo Kim Berg I just want to say: Wow!

I know that much more words are required to express my gratitude for the authors, my respect for their inspiring collaboration, my willingness to join and continue this ongoing process of the constant redefinitions of what solution focused practice in theory, description and practice means. EBTA definition task group decided to challenge issue of defining theory within solution focused practice. Keeping in mind aspects of theory, description and practice this paper clearly express it's "semi-fictional" (Hans Vaihinger concept from "As if" philosophy - Vaihinger, 1911) status of defining solution focused practice. Peter Sundman and the team, within EBTA task group, made a terrific attempt to describe a wide range of diversity within the SF approach, and put it into a kind of practice definition. We can see that authors followed rather inclusion of many practices, than exclusion of some explorations. Still it's worth to remember about Steve de Shazer tendency to describe his work by using statements as: "I do it", "I do that something" which were wide enough words to include potential diversity of SF styles of work. Steve de

Shazer once said in response to John Weakland's statement about getting to the Ericksonian essence (Hoyt, 2001):

> "When you start to look for the essence of the Erickson's work or brief therapy, you're always in danger of forgetting the 'nonessential' stuff. You automatically point to something that is nonessential when you say something is essential. Automatically. And you're in danger than of sticking something into the 'nonessential' box that will prove, in the long run, to be just essential as anything else has been."

Above lines help me to understand Theory of solution-focused practice paper as a given try to describe our solution focused approach as the map which is not the territory. Naturally all my comments in this review should also be treated in the same way.

One of the key aspect authors refer to is the role of the idea that solution focused practice is something more than the set of the questions, techniques of having conversations. In this case "more" means that professionals using solution focused approach, probably develop solution focused mind sets, at least partially, rooted in some theoretical systems. I was introduced personally by Luc Isebaert to the idea that SF approach is much more the way of thinking, than just the way of talking, or even asking only sf questions. Authors in respect to the history and to the process of developing approach have referred to some systems like: social constructivism, language philosophy or buddhist thinking. In fact diversity of applications, different streams within SF practice took also inspiration from other systems, like from stoicism philosophy, general semantics, Christian thinking, health psychology just to mention a few. My hope is that in coming future this richness of sources of inspiration will be explored much more.

Having in mind presented in the paper idea of the importance of the context I can clearly say that extracting human being from particular context means talking about totally different human being, one quite unreal, since in SF approach man should be always seen within context and within circular interaction between human being and the particular contexts. When I consider my practice, I can see focus on the context as something fundamental, and at the same time I would like to highlight importance of promoting idea of human being's functioning within contexts: external and internal ones at the same time. Our role is to usefully consider and utilize potential interactions within and between both types of this contexts. I see reasons for that also in Steve de Shazer and Insoo Kim Berg words that brief therapy is "a therapy organized around the context which people built for themselves and/or in which they find themselves" (de Shazer & Berg, 1995).

Authors present general definition of the solution-focused practice as: "Clients get support for change from a practitioner based on the client's resources, skills, strengths, future hopes and interaction within their environment." At least for me, this definition narrows some possibilities in everyday practice, which are also mentioned to some extent at the paper. One of the strategies I refer to is the usefulness of professional's perceptions, experience, knowledge and using "theories from social psychology, discursive psychology and systems theory", which authors openly mentioned. I propose another general definition of the solution-focused practice as "assisting clients in achieving what's wanted and chosen by them in certain situation on the basis of every necessary and ethical source of inspiration" (Switek, Panayotov, Strahilov, 2018).

Our SF world is full of statements about close listening to the clients and building solution-focused practice on getting from them feedback on what was useful during session. There's always a possibility that professionals using SF approach can value much more some theoretical systems, than client's suggestions. The same may happen when professionals treat some SF findings, conclusions developed for example in BFTC in Milwaukee or within Bruges Model, not as suggestions to explore and verify, but as basic SF tenets we have to follow during session. Authors remind us about risk in transforming solution-focused practice into solution-forced one. Keeping in mind idea of the context sensitivity we can say that shape of the solution-focused practice developed in different times, places, between different people might be seen by us only as the inspiration and that we're obliged to develop our solution-focused practice in our time, place and with our clients. My suggestion is that what basically we should learn from Milwaukee team is the way they choose to co-create solution focused practice, and such patterns we should apply at our contexts with hope for similar or different findings co-created with current clients.

Importance of the language is another fundamental aspect of the solution-focused practice mentioned by the authors. I can only support my colleagues in promoting importance of that issue within our practice. Since the topic is widely described within the paper in this review I'll refer only to a few aspects of the use of the language.

Authors propose line of thinking taken from the language philosophy where "solution focused practitioners rely on what might be called 'creative interaction', where meaning is created in life events between people and this is basis for solution-focused change" and they somehow present idea that "personal thoughts [...] do not have the controlling quality sometimes ascribed to them". I would gladly welcome in the future more reflections on solution-focused practice where meaning is created in life events between active parts of this events, which are located around and within the client. This is the place where idea about bridging external and internal contexts could apply quite practically. One of the propositions how can we describe and practice such is presented within BBraveC Model of the multi dimensional circularity of the motions (Switek, 2019).

Following some article lines we read "the focus on the conversation is on the interaction between people" and idea of "significant other" is proposed. My practice and feedback gathered from my client's feedback suggest that, at least sometimes, talking about relationship with "significant others" might be understood wider and involve "significant self" where client consider relationship with own "self". Also "significant other" might refer to the relationship with any other living beings, as well as, parts of the material world.

Another point which could be more described in the future is the aspect of understanding language. My impression is that authors mainly address language to verbal communication. Although it's clearly stated that "language is the key element in solution-focused practice" importance of the nonverbal communication could be enhanced and more addressed in the future descriptions. Sounds, movements, pictures, shapes and so on, during years of sf development were creatively incorporated into solution-focused practices.

Vision of the man, vision of the human being within solution-focused practice is full of hope, acceptance and kind of admiration. Indeed, we do value our clients and authors directly describe that stance presented by the side of the professionals who use solution-focused practice. That's one of the reasons we do work on the basis of what we see as client's resources. At the same time solution-focused tradition invites us to utilize dynamic language while we describe client's potentials. My wish is that while we promote importance of the language within our approach, we could combine it with the idea of using dynamic descriptions rather, than those based on valuing other people. We can read at the paper that clients "are resourceful, competent and resilient". From my point of view it's the common solution-focused language game, unfortunately a sad one, where we claim that we compliment our clients, that we work on the basis of their resources, and in fact we base our compliments on the pattern of valuing human beings. My point of view on this is clear and it says that valuing, labeling another person, even if it's done by complimenting in the form of assessing a person, is the use of the mechanism underlying racism, any discrimination based on making people "better or worse". I'd like to wait for the moment when, even in our SF world, it becomes unethical. What I do think is that "all" discriminations, including racism use patterns of valuing other people. By valuing I mean "defining nature of the person, identity", referring "labels". Often general pattern is based on "you're good vs. you're bad", "you're ok vs. not ok". Some can try to perform valuing toward positive "labels", like in SF many do, still it is the use of "valuing others pattern". In my delusions "valuing" is one of the backgrounds for discriminations, where I define someone as "good or bad" and in such situation it's easier to perform actions which can be seen as discrimination. I want to promote SF styles where we do stop "defining nature of others", where we do stop "valuing persons", even by using positive labels, since in my mind it's just one continuity, one "language game" and it's somehow "forgotten" Steve de Shazer's idea about describing clients with the use of dynamic languages, describing them through actions, potentials, not through, so called, nature.

Coming to some final remarks about wording. Presented paper refers to some dichotomies while describing solution-focused practice. Two basic dichotomies are: problem vs. solution, and problem talk vs. solution talk.

Historically it's quite easy to understand circumstances under which names as "problem" or "solution" were utilized within solution-focused vocabulary. Some of you may know that my work within so called solution focused practice ended up in sending names like "problems", "solutions", "problem talk" or "solution talk" for a kind of nice holidays. Instead of that I use wording like "unwanted", "less-wanted", "more-wanted", "wanted", and "useful talk", which can be understood, as common experience between professional and client co-created for the purpose of usefulness, which is defined as helpful in achieving what's wanted and chosen by the client.

I cannot simply resist to express my admiration to the authors, also because of the way they described key topics in solution-focused practice. It's a great idea to present our practice through the goals mainly, than from a tool perspective. Each of our interventions is meant for something. The purpose is much more dominant than the tool, the way we want to accomplish that purpose. Collection of the topics in solution-focused practice described at the paper seems to be absolutely sufficient, as long as, we remember that any topic, any experience which empower clients in achieving wanted situation, might be treated as integral part of our something-focused approach. We can ask questions, we can answer the questions, we can act in any ethical way, as long as, we all do our best to follow rules:

Continue what works!

When needed act differently!

Imagine what's wanted!

References

de Shazer, S. & Berg, I. K. (1995). The brief therapy tradition. In J. H. Weakland & W. A. Ray (Editors), Research Institute Propagations: Thirty years of the influence from the Mental (pp. 249-253). New York: Routledge.

Hoyt, M. F. (2001). A conversation with Steve de Shazer and John Weakland. In: Interviews with brief therapy experts, Philadelphia.

Switek, T., Panayotov, P., Strahilov, B., (2018). Making waves. Solution Focused practice in Europe. Sofia: EBTA.

Switek, T. (2019). BBraveC. Workshop presented at SFBTA conference, Montreal, Canada, 2019, http://www.centrumpsr.eu/wp-content/uploads/2019/12/BbraveC.pdf, Accessed, 31.7.2020.

Vaihinger, Hans (1911), Philosophie des Als Ob, Leipzig : F. Meiner.

Authors

Peter Sundman, BA, social worker, clinical supervisor, coach, licensed Solution Focused psychotherapy trainer, consultant, coordinator of the TaitoBa House Solution Focused net-work. Annankatu 29 A 12, 00100 Helsinki, Finland.
Email: peter.sundman@taitoba.fi

Matthias Schwab, MA, Psychologist, MA, Fine Art. Solution-focused therapist, coach, trainer and supervisor in private practice. Editorial board member of the Journal for Solution Focused Practices. Supporting "social sculptures" in working within the Free International University and the Solution-Focused Collective. Türkenstraße 3, 91522 Ansbach, Germany.
Email: matthias@the-void.org

Dr. Ferdinand WOLF, clinical psychologist, systemic Solution-focused psychotherapist in private practice, licensed systemic solution-focused psychotherapy trainer, supervisor and coach. Siget 61, A-7053 Hornstein, Austria.
Email: ferdinand@wolf.co.at

Marie-Christine Cabié, psychiatrist, medical director of an ambulatory and inpatient ward in Paris. Psychotherapist, trained and trainer in Family Therapy, SFT, Bruges Model, Ericksonian hypnotherapy. President of EBTA.
Email: mc.cabie@orange.fr

John Wheeler, MA, UKCP Registered Systemic Psychotherapist. Full member of Solution Focus in Organisations. Former member of board for EBTA. Former President IASTI. Former member of editorial board for Journal for Solution Focused Brief Therapy. Head of Centre for Solution Focused Trainers. External Lecturer with Newcastle University. 5 Runhead Gardens, Ryton. NE40 3HH. UK. Email: John@johnwheeler.co.uk

Rytis Pakrosnis, BA in Psychology, MA in Health Psychology, PhD in Social Sciences (Psychology), EuroPsy certified psychologist, Solution-focused practitioner in private practice and at Vytautas Magnus University Psychology Clinic, associate professor at Vytautas Magnus University (Kaunas, Lithuania), visiting professor at University of Warsaw (Poland), editorial team member for the Solution-Focused Literature journal and for for Frontiers in Health Psychology, former co-editor of the International Journal of Solution-Focused Practices. Biliuno g. 46, Kacergine, LT53447, Lithuania. Email: rytis.pakrosnis@vdu.lt

Michael Klingenstierna Hjerth, M.SC in psychology, BA in philosophy, Licensed Psychologist. Clinical psychologist, trainer and supervisor at Solutionwork Institute. Co-founder of Solutionwork Institute Stockholm, President of International Solution-Focused Training Institutes (IASTI), former secretary of EBTA, former editorial team member of International Journal of Solution-Focused Practices. Author of two books on solution-focus and neuropsychiatry. Segelflygsgatan 39, 12833, Skarpnäck, Sweden. Email: michael@solutionwork.se

Reviewers

Thorana Nelson, Ph.D., professor emerita of family therapy at Utah State University. Founding member and former secretary/treasurer of the Solution-Focused Brief Therapy Association. Prior to retirement, she enjoyed solution-focused training and supervision of solution-focused brief therapy. Author/editor of a number of SFBT books, including, Solution-Focused Brief Therapy With Families (Routledge, 2019).

Dr. Alasdair Macdonald, consultant psychiatrist for 30 years, registered family therapist and supervisor. Brief therapist for 25 years, solution-focused therapist since 1988. Publications in psychotherapy outcome and other interests. Previous office-bearer, European Brief Therapy Association. Former Medical Director; now freelance trainer and management consultant in China and elsewhere. Email: macdonald@solutionsdoc.co.uk

Arild Aambø, physician and senior advisor at the Norwegian Institute of Public Health. External Lectur-er at Oslo Univeristy and OsloMet. Founder of and from 1994 – 2004 leader of Workshop of Primary Health Care (PMV) in Oslo. Trainer in SFBT in collaboration with Berg and de Shazer in Norway and internationally. Published several articles and book-chapters on solution focused work, and a monograph on Solution Oriented Conversations (2004).

Sukanya Wignaraja (MSc Oxon), certified Solution-focused therapist and coach in private practice in Colombo, Sri Lanka. 75 Kynsey Road, Colombo 0800, Sri Lanka.
Email: wignaraja@gmail.com

Guy Shennan, therapist, trainer, consultant, specialising in solution-focused practice. Founding member of the UK Association of Solution Focused Practice. Founder of the Solution-Focused Collective. Social worker, past Chair of the British Association of Social Workers. 36 Shepton Houses, Welwyn Street, London E2 0JN, UK.
Email: guyshennan@sfpractice.co.uk

Switek Tomasz, MA in social prevention and rehabilitation, certified SF therapist, trainer and supervisor. Founder of the SFA Center, Poland. Board member of the EBTA and of the International Alliance of Solution-Focused Teaching Institutes (IASTI). Tomasz has created Situations Focused Open Model.
Email: tomaszswitek@centrumpsr.eu

CPSIA information can be obtained
at www.ICGtesting.com
Printed in the USA
LVHW111458210920
666678LV00002B/438